Survivor
Not
Statistics

By Lurleen Hilliard

Copyright © 2012
All rights reserved.
ISBN -10 1491077778
ISBN 13 - 978 1491077771
LLCN - 2013919913
Nolonger Victims ™

DEDICATION

This book is dedicated to every single Man, Woman and Child, who has ever lived a life of abuse. It is also in memory of all those that have died at the hands of their abuser, before they could escape.

They may be gone from our world, but they will never be forgotten.

INTRODUCTION

This is the true life story of myself and my family. It is one of those stories that in some way may hit home with a lot of people around the world, not just in Ireland, but it is time that the truth is told its time for us to stop been the Victims. As the longer we hide what goes on behind closed doors and the longer we stay quiet out of fear and intimidation, the more power we are giving those that are our abusers.

Take away their power, and you see them for what they truly are, small, weak excuses, for human beings. They were not born the way they act, they either acquired their mode of thinking by learned behavior or by been bullies and always getting away with their actions. In life we say it is easier to get rid of the victims rather than the bullies.

Abuse that is sometimes the worst to heal and to handle is not the physical, not the sexual or verbal abuse it is the Mental Abuse. You can hide the bruises, the scars, and you can put on the smile, but the mental abuse is some of the most traumatic in life to heal. I do not know whether or not it ever can be gotten rid of, as there will always be a trigger to remind you of something. This book is based on facts the only changes made to any details are the names of my family, and the exact towns and areas that we lived in.

The sole reason for this is that we have all suffered enough. My children like all kids who live in an abusive environment did not ask to be born, nor did they ask to lead the life that they did. We did not have a choice back then, but now we do and now I intend to protect them for the rest of their lives. And that is the only reason that these details are been changed. It is not to protect our abuser, it is rather to let him know, that despite all he did, we survived, we lived and are here to tell our story.

This book is dedicated to all the Women, Men and Children around the world, who are still victims of Domestic Violence and Abuse and or Rape. You are not alone, you survive every day of your life through sheer determination to escape from your life as you know it. If one person can be given the strength and courage to escape their abuser from reading this book, then it has been worth all the heartache that was endured in order to get here. Remember what you think about you bring about that is my motto in life now. The word Can't is not in my vocabulary, nor that of my children. You can do anything in life, once you believe that you can.

Imagine your life without your abuse in it and you will have it one day you just have to believe that you deserve it and that you can do it. You are not alone, despite what they tell you. Open your mouth, tell people about what is happening, because once you do then you immediately take away a huge portion of their control over you. Then you take control of your life back into your hands, it is not an easy road or a quick one it is a long hard road, but one hell of a prize at the end of it.

You take your life and control over your life and that of your children's back from the grips of your abuser. Then he/she is seen for who they really are in life, a sad pathetic bully. You no longer simply exist in life you are ready now to live it and to enjoy it. Life is for living and as a survivor of abuse irrespective of what form it took you now have a lot of making up to do for the lost years, when you were a victim of abuse, as a victim you had no choice in life. But as a survivor every choice is now yours to make.

ACKNOWLEDGEMENTS

There is not enough space to thank everybody, however I would like to say a special thank you to the following people. In the USA I have to thank Rebecca, Turner, Heidi, Chris, Al, Craig, Kathy, Gladys, Pedro, Didi, Janet. You gave me the strength and determination to do this book, I am indebted to you all. I would also like to thank Luke Tyrell who has been an amazing friend to one of my sons, no matter what he has been there for him .Dermot Mc Namara from Mc Namara Solicitors in Ireland has been a huge support, legally for me and was always available to help when any issue arose.

In Ireland I would like to thank all that have supported us, however a special word of thanks must go to the following people. Lorraine Farrell & Deirdre Ormond from The Windmill Medical Center, Joanne Moore, Lorraine Weldon, Sara Weldon, Anne Mc Inerney. My godmother Molly Maher who was always there with a listening ear and a cup of tea. I also want to thank Eddie Kirk, Marie Geraghty and Laoisaigh Kelly. And my boys I would not be who I am today without their support. I also big thank you to Yolanda Ryan in Gibraltar a friend who is more like my sister.

A very special Thank You must go to Cathy Kelly, who is one of Irelands most famous and respected authors. Cathy kindly offered to endorse this book cover for me, and it is an honor to have had her do this. I hope to make her proud with the end product of the book. Since beginning to write this book, I have made some amazing Friends that are now more family then friends, and they are far too many to mention. The majority of them are in the USA and all are on the Nolonger Victims (Lurleen) Facebook page, which I set up to help all victims of abuse, irrespective of their gender or abuse. In particular those that have done so much behind the page, that I would not be as strong as I am now had she and all the others not supported me unconditionally. A special word of thanks goes to Brenda Plumley who has supported this book and all that I do below and with my dream for the future.

Nolonger Victims is also on all the social network sites and Linkedin for anybody to connect up with me. Not forgetting the Minxanator who is inspirational to all .My two sons that are with me are my life, and I would be lost without their support and love. If it was not for one of these two we would not be alive today, as he was and is our protector from our abuser. My son who has been alienated from me for two years I love with all my heart and I hope that in time he will realize that the truth is in this book and the truth has to be told.

Finally I have been very lucky to be involved with many organizations across the USA who work tirelessly to make the voices of not just the children of abuse, but teenagers, men, women seniors, veterans basically everybody that can be a victim of abuse has at least one voice out there for them. Whether you are a man, woman or child if you have been abused then you don't have to suffer in silence. Having the opportunity to speak on air on numerous occasions with Stephen Roberts from the USA but across the world, working with CARI Child Abduction Recovery International and linking with all the Law Enforcement agencies and individuals that have helped to make the voices of all victims of all abuses heard, is what has helped to give me the strength to not just tell my story but to be proud of the fact that I survived and am here to tell the tale, whilst helping with others through collaboration as many as possible to live life rather than to exist in it.

TABLE OF CONTENTS

Dedications

Introductions

Acknowledgements

Chapter 1   Childhood

Chapter 2   Downward Spiral

Chapter 3   Road-trip

Chapter 4   Life of Abuse

Chapter 5   My Daughter

Chapter 6   The Killer Affair

Chapter 7   The Devil Appears

Chapter 8   Life Back in Ireland

Chapter 9   Rory Becomes His Dad

Chapter 10   Jake My Miracle

Chapter 11   Vegas – The Chef & His Prodigy

Chapter 12   Signs of An Abusive Personality

Chapter 13   Are You a Victim? Escape Now

Chapter 14   Worldwide Centers of Help

Chapter 15   What The Future Holds Now

CHAPTER 1 – CHILDHOOD

I was born in the late 1960s to very hard working parents, like many, many parents of that time they had lived and worked in the USA for years prior to my birth. In actual fact, I had an older sister who was still born in New York, the sad thing is, that in those days even though she was full term, it was a stigma so the babies were taken and put into graves that in general were not even marked. So as much as I would love to find her grave, I doubt I ever will. My mam told me that I was a miracle baby she was very religious, and went to Mass every-day she did her novenas to get pregnant with me. I never knew the reason as to why I was such a miracle baby but perhaps if I had of known, I would not have lost so many babies myself in similar circumstances to my mam.

However it was a totally different life back then and some things just were not spoken about. My parents had left for New York in 1961 my dad was a mechanic worked three jobs and my mam worked for the airline at the time Pan Am. They lived in Texas as well as New York and when they had saved enough money, they came home to Ireland they bought their own house where they both lived till their deaths. They invested the money they had made wisely in a garage business, dad sold the cars, did the mechanics and mam she dealt with all the paperwork and the customers.

It sounds idyllic reading this back, but they had their problems numerous times world war 3 would break out at home, but my dad never raised his hand to my mam or abused her in any-way that I am aware of, it just was not done. I did not grow up in a violent atmosphere nor in an abusive one, now I see that I actually grew up in a very good home. When I was born they put me onto their passport at the time and brought me back to America to see all their family and friends there. At this time in Ireland they would have been viewed as the wealthy, as to fly from Ireland to New York for a ten day holiday in the 60s cost a lot of money and was not something that was done by many. I since found out that they did this as they both had their own green cards for the USA,I still have dads, but by bringing me over there on their passports, they assumed that it would include me onto their green cards. This is a point I am currently verifying but I am hoping is very much the case. As children we view our parents as gods, we want for nothing and if they have it, then they give it to us. They teach us values in life, how to treat and respect others and how to behave. My parents were very strict on me, suppose been the oldest I had to be the one that had all the boundaries to test. I subsequently had a brother and an adopted sister. However they are both dead to me   due to their actions towards my family and me. My friends are now our real family now.

I also had another little brother who was again still born also at full term, I have no idea as to how my mam was able to handle the birth and burial of two of her children, it really shows her mental strength at the time. Perhaps that is where I got my determination from. Although most people say I am the image of my dad and in most ways I was a real daddy's little girl. We were very close, so close that he died in my arms, in my bed some years ago. And as hard as that was it was, it was also a wonderful moment, as he was the first person to hold me when I was born into this world, yet I was the last person to hold him in my arms, when he was leaving our world. It is a very special moment that I will always hold with me.

Growing up was normal I suppose, nothing special I went to school I hated school and in general was useless in school, especially at exams, I would just freeze .But what I did learn in school and in general about myself, mainly as a teenager, was if you showed me what had to be done, or told me what you wanted, then I did not have a problem doing it, and it would be done perfectly. I had only ever one dream in school and that was to work in the Travel Industry, god I remember going into Dublin city with my best friend who lived next door to me, on a Saturday and we would always end up coming home with me carrying piles of travel brochures. I would   hide in my room or sit on the loo and have pretend discussions with pretend customers over their holidays. It sounds crazy now but no matter how many career guidance teachers told me that it was a bad field or that I would not make it, I proved them wrong. I did and I worked as not only a general travel agent for years but also as a corporate agent and to this day still love travel and airports. I even won Ms. Travel Trade in 1990, so I must have been doing something right.

I think that there is something inside me that loves to go to new Places and to live there, not just for a holiday, but to really live there and to experience the life of other people around the world. It has rubbed off on at least two of my children, as they love to travel and to enjoy lots of adventures. Some of what we have done will give them memories for a lifetime, and considering that they will have so many horrible memories of their childhood, it helps to know that there are now also the good ones of recent years, and that is what they will I hope remember more of in life.

CHAPTER 2 – DOWNWARD SPIRAL

Downward spiral, this is the only words that I can even consider thinking about that would ever describe my life from the day I met my ex-husband, to the day that I decided to be a survivor. The day I met him was the biggest mistake of my life, and one that I have lived to regret. But the day I got the guts to tell the world about him and to realize that I am better than him, and that I do not need or want him or his abuse in my life, is the day that I became a survivor and I became me again.

Now don't get me wrong I have a very long way to go, there are things that I have gone through, things that I do not know if they will ever be able to be wiped from my brain, but these are things that I am working on and someday, I don't know when, but someday I will be free from all his pain and hurt and that is what I aim for every day of my life.

I was not anything special growing into a teenager I was very chubby, very self- conscious, god if any male even said hello to me, I would go fifty shades of red, probably make a fool of myself and stutter and splutter my words. But in hindsight, I suppose I did lead a sheltered life and perhaps that was my down-fall ,as when I met my ex he was everything that my parents did not want for me. So the more they said they did not like him or that they did not want to have me going out with him the more I stood my ground, if only I had listened to them, but hindsight is an amazing thing.

However if I had not of met my ex and ended up marrying him, then I would not have had my children, so that is the only good thing that I can honestly say came out literally of my ex-husband. I was only 19 years old, working my dream job in a top Travel Agency. I was getting to travel the world for free, as at that time working in travel had lots of bonuses, not like our world today. I had been given my first car by my parents on the understanding that I would never ever drink and drive and to this day that has always stuck with me. It is something that my 18 year old son is so adamant about, even with his own friends that it makes me proud, as it is an inexcusable action that causes catastrophic pain to many.

I lived in a big city in Ireland and he lived in a small rural town where everybody knew everybody and if you were an outsider well you would always be an outsider. They all knew your business who you were, what you drove, what you wore, it thankfully now has changed and this treatment is not that common, but back then it was horrible. You always felt like you were been watched or judged and to this day, that same town although now a lot bigger, is still the same. The same few people talk behind everybody's backs, they bitch, they moan, but to your face they are as nice as pie. I used to get angry at these people, but now I just pity them, as I'd rather be me and be straight and get into trouble for not putting my brain into gear a lot before I open my mouth, but at least those that are my friends are my friends. We are all open and straight to each other. It should not matter what you have in your bank account or what you drive, it is the person that counts and thankfully those that are in my life can count on me, and I can count on them.

Without them I would not have got through so much, they know who they are, I am not going to name them, as it is not my right to put them into my book, but for years they would tell me to leave, I just didn't have the strength, but when I did they were waiting there with their arms open and still are to this day. I was a tomboy even though I worked in the Travel and Airline industry, it was apparently a glamorous job to have, at home or out with my friends it was jeans and shirts. I had mainly lads as my friends at this time, and that's all we were, friends, my best friend had at such a young age been in an abusive relationship, and she packed her bags and left Ireland, she went to England and then ended up in Australia where she is still to this day, and is happily married to a great guy and has her own children now.

But the lads were my buddies, we hung out, we went out, we had fun and they were protective of me. When I first saw my ex, I was actually with the lads at a racetrack in the city, we would go there at the weekends or up to the north of Ireland to see car racing .It was harmless fun, just teenagers growing up. For the sake of using a name I will call my ex Bas, short for bastard, one that I think is suitable. Bas was the James Dean of the group, he was the cool one to always look good he was good looking, I can't take that from him, he was funny and cheeky and all the girls flirted with him. Me I stood in the background, id only stutter or make fool of myself, but one day he noticed me at the track, he was been chatted up by some girl who I still remember, as she had really bad acne and I felt so sorry for her. He wanted her to think that he had a girlfriend, so he put his arm around me and that was the start of the next 23 years of my life. Little did I know that he actually did have a girlfriend at the time, he just never told me, the lies and the games had now sadly started and the sadly lasted over 20 yrs.

I was a virgin when I met him I was not one for sleeping around, in Actual fact I am still not a woman who sleeps around, it is just not me. He asked me out for a drink that Sunday, but my mates and I had a rule, if we went out together, we went home together, I was the one driving, so I said no maybe another time. He went off and that was that or so I thought. A few days later one of the lads sisters called up to see me, she told me that Bas had been in an accident and had nearly been killed. I was worried sick it was before mobile phones so I did not know how to contact him, I was told he was at home but was in a bad way. I spoke to my mam she didn't know him at this time but she told me that maybe I should go down to where he lives and to see if he was ok.

This was going to be the hardest thing I had ever done, as me who goes red and stutters or splutters if a guy said hello, was going uninvited to his house, but I got the guts and went there. It should have been the kick in the butt that I needed to realize that he was a player, but like a fool I ignored the signs. His dad opened the door to their family home and told me that he wasn't there, that he was up playing pool in the village pub. I asked him was he not injured and he told me that he was lucky to be alive, but that he wanted to get out of the house.

I left my name and number. I suppose hoping he would call. Well he left me to sit and stew for two days before he called, and as I didn't have their house number, I just had to wait. But call he did and we spoke for hours on the phone and again the next day and the next night .After a few days he asked me to meet him for a date, the following Sunday at his house and then to go to a pub in the next town for a few drinks, so I agreed .I was in shock for want of a better word, as this was the cool guy in the town, the Mr. Popular and he was asking me Ms. Frumpy for a date, it made me more confident and I felt important, stupid yes, but how many of us as teenagers have not had that feeling at some-stage. When the Sunday arrived I drove to his house and nearly died, when I walked in, as the entire family where there all the brothers, sisters, in-laws, nieces, nephews, it was my worst nightmare. They weren't there for me, it was just a coincidence they were there for their usual Sunday lunch and drinking the homemade wine, one of his brothers would make, which was lethal, it was so potent. Anyway after all the introductions we left and we went to the pub. I was driving so only wanted cokes to drink, he was making smart comments about been a cheap date, but I let them in one ear and out the other. After a few hours there the place was really buzzing, the music was blaring and everybody was having fun, but there was a girl on the other side of the lounge that was giving me dirty looks.

I didn't know her, I had never been to that pub before ,after sometime when we went to leave, she approached Bas on our way out and started an argument with him .I was years later to find out that she was actually his girlfriend up until he met me. And indeed was involved with her behind my back, whilst with me and 22 years later, I find out that she had been pregnant with his daughter at the time of the incident in the pub. Although to my knowledge DNA was never done he has said she is his daughter, and the two boys with me have met her twice now. We left the pub and went to a chipper for a bag of chips, suppose it was a cheap date, but we had fun and we were getting on well. When I dropped him home later that night, he kissed me and from then on we were a couple.

Over the following weeks he would be on the phone non- stop when not working as a welder, or he would be out with me. We would just get into the car and drive to god knows where, we were young and carefree. I'd get tickets for travel and we would go to London for the day or Paris, it must have seemed like he fell on his feet when he met me, but I certainly didn't. The girl that he had been involved with made our life hell, she would turn up at any pub that we were in, it was like she had a tracking device on him or somebody was telling her where we were, and there would always be a scene. Then the threats started, she would ring my place of employment, she would tell me that she had been sleeping with him the night before, when on some occasions he had stayed at my house on the couch or I at his, so I knew that this wasn't true.

She would tell me that I would be dead, that she would do this that and the other to me, but then I heard that she was in hospital in a town nearby that was for people with mental health problems. This is what Bas even told his own mam whom I was very close to. He told us that her dad and brothers had asked him to go and to talk to her to try to calm her down, as she couldn't handle their break up. What he failed to tell me was that she was apparently pregnant with his baby. She called one particular night to his mams house I was there, he was in the bath and his mam read the girl the riot act and ran her solely cause she and I believed the story her son had said to us.

His mam was a lady, a great mam, and a great grandmother so for her to speak as she did to this girl, was very out of character. If she thought that she was pregnant with her grandchild the knitting needles would have been out, and she would have had the child in the families lives whether Bas liked it or not. But like me she was taken for a fool and died not knowing what her youngest son was truly like although, she had an idea. On one occasion Bas asked me to bring him to the National Maternity Hospital in Dublin and to wait outside for him, as she was in having some tests and he had been asked to go see her. When the truth was, she had just had a baby apparently his first born daughter. After this he wanted to get away from the town, he wanted to travel, to go anywhere, but where he was living at that time. So we decided that in a few months we would leave our jobs and travel around Europe, the idea then came to us to buy an old banger of a car for 50 IRL a lot at the time and we built it into an amazing car that would take us on an adventure to lots of different countries.

On this adventure not only did I get pregnant, but we got caught up in the civil war in Yugoslavia, just as it was starting and then the fall of communism in Bulgaria, when we were trying to get home to Ireland.

CHAPTER 3 – ROAD TRIP

The excitement of travelling around the Europe free of any rules or restrictions may as well have been the world to us, it was unreal. We were going to be away for months with no parents, no rules, just to do what we wanted and when we wanted, we felt so grown up planning this trip. We were to go from Rosslare to Calais then drive thru France and subsequently into Austria, Greece, Turkey, Bulgaria, Crete, Albania, Leicheinstein, Switzerland, Yugoslavia. The day we were leaving for Rosslare we got delayed, so even though Bas drove like a lunatic way above the speed limit, when we arrived into Rosslare, the ship was pulling away. So we had to stay overnight in a hotel and get the next ship. We didn't mind though as Ireland was at the time in the world cup, it was 1990 so the buzz in the town and the hotel was great, finally we got onto our ship and we went on our trip.

We did all the scenic and tourist things in France and Paris we went to Trocadero so many times. I still love that place to this day, as the skater's and the smell of the chestnuts been roasted, and the crepe freshly cooking, is one that clings to your memories for life. We drove through the mountains into Austria, we stayed in a camp on the top of the mountains in France, it was surreal to have driven from the sun in our shorts and tops to now be in a campsite where there is snow.

On our way down the mountain into Austria, the clutch went on our steep descent, I have never ever been so afraid in my life. To be coasting the car down the mountain side, with nothing either side of the road we were on except sheer drops of thousands of feet has kept me to this day terrified of heights and roads that have no barriers. Somehow, someway, somebody was looking out for us as we made it to safety. When we made our way into Yugoslavia, it was like a different world, the poverty, the people, it was hard to believe that these countries all bordered each other, yet were millions of miles apart in their lives and their economy.

We stopped at this petrol station on the top of a hill, it was very remote, I don't even think that they knew where Ireland was. Anyway we didn't have any of their currency, so they traded a full tank of petrol for two leather cowboy hats that we had bought at the market in Paris,it was a fair trade even if we came out of it the better end. At the time we knew very little about Yugoslavia, it was not somewhere that was spoken about much in Ireland and we were to soon find out why.

Our car broke down as soon as we arrived into Bosnia, it didn't help that it was July 4th and they were celebrating American Independence. The town and city was all closing early and we didn't speak their language, we didn't know who to ask for help. I then decided that I would approach a police man who told us to go to the police station, but he sent us through the roughest and most dangerous area of the city and in the wrong direction. Later we found out that although the city was celebrating American Independence, a lot of its people were communists and didn't like Westerners. I think I at the time jinxed myself, as we were so scared about been mugged or worse that I put my bag with all our stuff in it down the front of my dungarees, and pretended that I was pregnant .Little did I know that I actually was pregnant with my eldest son who is now 22 years old.

Eventually we found a small garage where a man had said that he could help us with the car, it at this stage needed a new alternator. So he took Bas with him, in his little Robin Reliant three wheeler car and told me that they would be back in a while, that they were going to get the part and to fix it when they returned. They left me there in the car in the sweltering heat, with no form of communication and with all these men who worked in the yard and the factory beside it walking over to the car to look at me it was so scary. I sat in that car bursting for the loo, with the window barely open for over 5 hours before they came back. The man who had taken Bas off wasn't a con artist, he was genuinely trying to help, however his car was pretty old and very basic.

On the way up the motorway, his bonnet blew up into the air and he Couldn't see where he was going, at the same time he was going up the hill to the motorway, an oil tanker was coming down it, both on the same side of the road. He opened his own driver door and got Bas to open his and to both hold and close down the bonnet of the car, they just about managed to do it, as the tanker past them by, but the wind caught the bonnet, and it got ripped off as did his driver door. So he came back without his bonnet and without his door, I couldn't help but laugh. As soon as the car was fixed, we left and went to leave Yugoslavia. I have to say at that time despite the turmoil in the country, the scenery was amazing the boardwalks over the sea were just so beautiful and with the mountains in the background it was a sight that I hadn't seen before.

As we were driving south, we drove through this rural area only to realize that we had driven through an army checkpoint. When we looked into the rear view mirror, we had an army tank driving after us, positioning his gun, needless to say we jammed on and reversed pretty dam fast. When we were cleared from here, we took some wrong road and ended up behind a horse and cart with a local wedding party on it, but the weird thing was it was in Albania which was a closed country at the time. We stayed behind the wedding then got out of there as fast as possible.

After a lot of driving we ended up in Greece, I have never seen so many funny cars in my life, they had cars welded together, you could have a ·Ford Fiesta as the front of the car and a Ford Escort car at the back, different colors and just welded in place. It was like the Flintstones. We decided to board a ferry to Crete, and we went on all I can describe as a cattle ship, although it was a passenger ferry it was so over packed and crammed with people and cars it was hard to believe that we actually made it there alive. After arriving into Heraklion, we drove to Chania a small fishing village, we rented a small villa there and got settled in, although when we went to the shop and saw dog hanging up for sale, it sort of turned me my stomach. We were running short of money, so we were planning on killing a huge chicken that was running around the garden, we chased him or should I say Bas chased him for hours with a hatchet, he couldn't catch him, but then we saw he was actually a she and had little chicks, so we dropped that plan and went back to good old bread and butter.

I started to get sick here and we were really struggling for money so we decided to head home. The quickest route was to go via Turkey up into Bulgaria then over to France, but the best plans don't always work out. We got to Turkey it was a nightmare but we got through it into Bulgaria. We paid the visas on entry at the border however they did not tell us that our visas were only transit that we had to be out within 24 hours this was something we found out the hard way. Bulgaria was totally communist at this time, it was so depressing, so upsetting, that it is something that will stay with me for life. We ended up in Sofia the capital and went and booked a cheap room into a hotel beside the government buildings. When we walked out of the hotel, we were met by people been hosed down by water cannons, they were demonstrating against the communist regime, it was terrifying they didn't care who they hit with the cannons, they just wanted to cause chaos. The next day the same protestors blew up part of the government building this was our cue to leave. But anytime we wanted to speak to our family at home, we had to use hotel phones that were censored we later found out. We were cut off at every-time we mentioned what was happening outside the hotel.

There were queues outside shops for bread, than another shop for fruit so on and so forth it was a different world. We were taken aside by a manager in the hotel who worked for the underground he told us that our visas were expired, that this meant we could be arrested for been in the country and that we could like others disappear. Through many phone calls we managed to get word home that we needed help to escape, the hotel hid us in a room that was in the attic. By this stage I couldn't eat or drink, I had not been able to for days, nobody wanted to help us other than this manager but he could not be seen to be helping us or he would be killed there and then. After walking streets and literally asking people for help as they went by us, a man well dressed with a beard approached us and asked us if we needed help. He spoke English with an accent. By some miracle it turned out that he was a doctor ill call him Vladimir, he told us to go back to the hotel that he would be in contact .That evening he arrived there, he told me that I needed to get to a hospital, but to get home first. He gave us a set of maps which I still have, hand written with details of how to escape without been caught, through taking certain traffic-lights and turns .However before we did this we got word that there were flight tickets for us at the airport. We knew we would have to leave the car and that was another problem as the police wouldn't allow us to but we decided to just park it and get the flights.

When we left Bulgaria eventually this doctors father lost his job, then was taken off into the woods and was left for dead by the powers that be, as nobody in their country was allowed to help in
particular Westerners. So although he was a doctor he risked his life to help us, to this day we are still in touch with him although it is

separately now that we keep in contact. He escaped his old life there, for many years he could not return to see his parents or family. Thankfully he is now married with his own family and living a very successful life in the United States of America .I can honestly say that we owe our lives to this man and his kindness, he was at the time one in a million, as nobody else cared or wanted to know us. At Sofia Airport we met a female Hitler, she was unreal, she man-handled me and Bas and took all our money. She took anything of value from us, than they separated us. There is an article which I also have that was in a Bulgarian Newspaper after this incident at the airport ,as I went crazy at this lady ,and apparently it is not something that was done at the time.

I was sent to one area with some of my bags and Bas was taken away. I was ushered onto the plane alone and put near the front of the airplane, but then two men wearing trench coats like in a James Bond Movie sat either side of me, watching every move I made .I subsequently found out from the air hostess that these two were KGB. Somehow I had to escape them. So I asked to be moved to the front row of seats, it was empty and I lay across them as I was sick and it gave me time to plan. My flight was going to Paris but there are two airports there so I knew that I would have to lose these men. As soon as the flight landed I got my bags and I bolted, I ran and I ran I have no idea as to how but I lost them in the airport. After all the KGB couldn't really cause a scene in another countries airport, so I got to Charles De Gaulle. Air France gave me a free bus ticket and I managed to get my flights changed and flew directly to Dublin, I was immediately brought to the Mater Hospital, where I had a bleeding ulcer and found out I was pregnant.

Where Bas was I didn't know at this stage, but the Department of Foreign Affairs got involved, he was eventually brought home to Ireland. From that day on we basically lived together as a couple but a change had occurred in him and it was one that was to destroy mine and my sons lives, for what seemed like an eternity.

CHAPTER 4 – LIFE OF ABUSE

Finding out that I was pregnant was a shock, as much as I loved Babies and at some-stage in my life I wanted them, this was not the time. I was only 21 years old it was meant to be my time to enjoy life, to work, have fun and to make something of my life, but I was pregnant and that was that .I did at one stage think that I might have an abortion as I didn't know if I was ready for a baby. But I couldn't think further than the initial thought of that, as to me a baby doesn't ask to be made and it is something to treasure not to blame, so then came the task to tell my parents.

My mam was the first that I told of my parents, my dad I knew it would break his heart and I didn't know what to say or how to say it. So Bas initially told my mam and then went home in my car to his own house, he stayed across the road from my house for a few hours just in-case world war three broke out. But my dad just went to bed then my mam wouldn't talk to me, so I went to bed myself and cried for hours. I wasn't crying at the fact that I was pregnant, I think it was more the fact that all that had happened over the previous few months whilst abroad suddenly hit me, and now I was going to be a mam myself. But I feared how I would do this as with no home of my own, no money and no job it was going to be hard. I knew my parents would help me, but it wasn't exactly what I'd wanted.

After a few days my dad called a meeting with Bas, myself and mam, it was to ask him his intentions with me. My dad was very old fashioned in some ways and traditional. He told us that he would help us and even offered to build on a small flat to their house so that we had somewhere to live. As disappointed as he was in me he was still my dad and he still wanted to take care of me, even if I was going to be a parent myself. Unfortunately this is when I started to realize that going to mass everyday like my mam did and helping unmarried mams in poor areas of the city was all for show it wasn't really sincere. As mam was so afraid of what the neighbors would say and or the gossips. That really hurt me, to think that she was more worried about them, then she was of me and my life which had been changed forever. Our relationship from that day forward changed forever and it is something that I wish could have been reversed. But too much was said and done to mend it, so that it was like before. There is a saying that I used to hear a lot and that was love is like blue china costly such a rare, when broken can be mended but the cracks are always there and it sadly was too true with mam and I. We told Bas parents and family but they weren't shocked, as to be honest most of his brothers or sisters had at this stage had babies out of wedlock, so it was just another grandchild to look forward to. His mam who I will call Angel, as she was an angel to me from the day I met, her took me into her home when my mam threw me out. She just couldn't handle the fact that I was pregnant out of wedlock, it was too embarrassing for her and it was like id let her down. Angel took me in, she was so good to me, she started to knit cardigans and I still have them to this day, she was such a wonderful lady in every sense of the word. Yet her life had been such a hard one, that it really hurt me to see how she struggled in life and how she was living a life of abuse. In her words she had lived it for over 40 years.

She was of the era though of staying put and not walking away, she herself had seven children and was a wife and a mam hence as to why she stuck it out. But in the years that followed we got very close and one of the things that she said to me when we were alone, was to promise her that I wouldn't live my life like hers and waste 40 years on regret. Despite the fact that at this stage the real abuse hadn't started, she knew she saw the signs, I only wish that I had of seen them too. When my first son was born of course it was one of the best moments of my life, although later on in life I really wondered if I had done the right thing by having him, as he sadly has become his dad in every sense of the word. But although the signs for him were there for years, in his case I truly believe that it was like his dad learned behavior. However in saying that, as bad as Bas own father was he never stooped to the levels that his son did with me.

Bas escalated the abuse he had seen as a child to an entirely new level and to be honest this scares me, as I am afraid if the escalation continues in my oldest son that he will be even more abusive than his dad, and that is an extremely scary scenario. After our son was born in 1991 we moved closer to where my parents lived, this was for two reasons. The first that my dad had given Bas a job in his garage, so that we had some income and secondly as he was also going back to school it was on a bus route, I could also then go back to work at the same time. I worked full time during the day, he would mind our son then he would work the evening shifts.

Sometimes I even worked them with him, going from my job in Travel to the garage but it had to be done and that was life. Our rent at the time was IRL 300 a month and I remember how we thought that it was so much money as it was to us. My dad would lend me his van or a car from the garage, usually unknown to my mam as she didn't want anything to do with us and wouldn't help at all. My son we will call him. Rory was nearly two years old before she really started to get involved in his life and she missed out on so much, but dad he was always there. He was the one who would babysit for us or would sneak me up some extra cash that he had won at the races. He loved his horses and greyhounds and would throw me some extra money whenever he had it.

Mam couldn't stand Bas at this stage, even though she knew that we now had a child her grandchild together. She couldn't forgive him for nearly costing her their home and their livelihood that they had built up from scratch .In some-ways I really wish id listened to her but teenagers don't, they have to learn their own mistakes and to make those decisions, that as parents we know are wrong .But sometimes they have to find out the hard way as I and my children did. You see the lies and deceit had already started even whilst I was pregnant, I was too in love or so I thought to see it. I just thought that all that was been said and done was out of malice when in actual fact it was the truth and it was these facts that I should have taken listened to.

One night while I was pregnant, with only two weeks left to the due date and Bas was staying with me up at my family home just in case I went into labor. This particular night his friend called him to ask him to collect him and some other people from a 21_{st} party in a town close to where he lived. He didn't tell me that he was going the keys were on the hall table. I assume I dozed off and he just took them and went. He had car insurance from his job, so if he did drive my car I was always told that he was insured. It was a freezing cold icy night when I was woken in the middle of the night by my dad shouting at me, that there had been a crash and that Bas had been in it.

I didn't realize till this moment that he was even gone from the house. I went and took dads car and very heavily pregnant drove to the outskirts of the town where the crash had happened, the roads were full of black ice and I was terrified driving them. When I got there I saw what was left of my car in a tree stump and no Bas then I heard my name been called and a lady came out of her house up the road a bit to say that he was there. When I got to him I could see that his shoulder was gone on one side it was totally dislocated and broken, he told me that the others had gone home and that some had gone to the hospital. We went to his friend, as they were apparently expecting us. I was shocked and stunned by what I was met with. I was told by the sister of his friend that I was to say that I was driving the car for insurance purposes. I refused to as I wasn't even in the car, I was at home in bed and it was my parents business insurance, so I was not going to put myself into a situation that I couldn't get out of.

That was the last time that his so called friend spoke to me. He went to the hospital and was treated for his injuries, later released to go home to my parent house as I was still due the baby any day. One of the people in the car came up the next day to the house after going to the garage to see my car, and told me that only for the good driving of Bas that he would be dead. Funny when the color of money flashed before his eyes, he subsequently changed his story. I was told that the car skidded on black ice and he lost control. I wasn't told that he had been drinking and to this day don't know if he was, but in hindsight I would assume that he was, as he was later to be an alcoholic.

This was the start of his lies. My parents nearly lost their entire life savings, their house ,their business, everything over the claims made by the people in the car. It was all about money and greed they thought that my parents would simply pay up, it didn't go their way and they got nothing from my parents. This was the reason as to why my mam for over two years totally cut herself out of our lives as she couldn't stand Bas and what he stood for or for what he had done. Over time he finished his schooling and he then started to work full-time for my dad. I was still working in the city and would four nights a week, also go straight to dads business to work, the wages were not the best, a shift was six hours and it was just IRL15 per shift. But it was a total of an extra 30 IRL per night and that was a lot of money. He would come home and pretend to go over to the chipper, but he was really going to the pub, his lies started here in this house. I was naive and stupid at the time to not see through him, but sometimes when you are so close to something it is hard to see what is right in front of you. His affairs started here too, he would say he was going to the gym or to work when he wasn't he was off with another woman. He treated women like commodities and we were all there for his enjoyment, irrespective of the cost to us or our families. I suppose this was the start of the brainwashing.

After a few years in this house my parents helped us to get a deposit for a house, he was now working full time. Thanks to my dad again, who had paid for him to do courses in driving of trucks and oil tankers and in doing what is now known as the Hazchem certificate. It is what anybody who drives tankers or trucks around the world, that transports hazardous materials must have to ensure that they are qualified to handle any situation. Without my dad he would have had and been nothing and his way of repaying dads generosity was to destroy his daughters and his grand-children lives. It just shows what a total piece of scum he was basically from the day he was born.

We bought a three bed detatched house in a new estate that was been built, about ten minutes from my parents. It was close to the motorway to his own home town and handy for work. Thanks to the wages from his work driving the oil tankers we managed to buy our first car, god we were so proud of it. Our house we cherished, we kept it well and were always trying to upgrade it and make it a proper home for our children. In 1994 just after we moved into this house our second child was born, he was an extremely sick baby whilst I was pregnant and then when born. He was in and out of hospital so much that I ended up having to give up my career that I had worked so hard to achieve. But been a part time mam wasn't possible, my son needed me and I have never regretted my decision to give up my career for him. If it wasn't for him, I wouldn't be alive today.

Bas was I think jealous initially of the attention that our son was getting from me, as it was now really obvious about his temper. It was when my son was only very young that his abuse and his affairs started .Of course at first I believed the lies, the working late, the shifts down the country, the always looking really clean and smart and the presents. I was forever been given jewelry, in time I realized that these were only to try and ease his conscience to make him think that he was really a decent family man, when the reality was that he was instead an abusive bully who was having affairs with his co-workers.

We didn't really have much of a social life as it was hard to get babysitters, but when we could my parents would mind the kids and we would go for a meal. Really I suppose I should say I didn't have much of a social life, as he was having a whale of a time. He arrived home one night with a girl that I subsequently called multi colored eyes, as she had contacts in, but she would change the colors of her eyes with them hence the nick-name. He told me that she lived close by about a five min drive and that she worked in the office of the firm he worked for. He was helping to give her a lift to and from work so she was happy to babysit for us in return. What he failed to tell me was that he was having an affair with her, and the two of them would get together as much as possible, literally everyday including on their way to and from work, and me well id be nice and friendly to her for babysitting the unknowing wife.

Well after sometime I realized that he was spending less time at home, and that every word he said would have her name in it. I was so sick of hearing the name Ann. He would get birthday or valentines cards from work and they would always have love Ann on them, were as all others would just have from, so I knew that something was going on. I confronted him about it and he tried to lie his way out of it, but I kept at it, kept at him as I knew there was more to tell, that's one of the first times when he really hit me. I remember smashing a bottle of wine that he had been given onto the floor and storming out of the house, he had looked at me as if I was the one in the wrong instead of him. I walked for hours, I went to a local shopping center and was just walking around in a daze eventually I went home he was in bed asleep.

So much for the conscience, she didn't offer to babysit after that However, I did phone her and let her know that I knew all that was going on between her and Bas, she tried to deny it but the lies were tripping her up. She was not as good as he was at hiding the truth. Sometime later she left the company and went onto another job. Then he started to get more secretive, a lot more devious and would have knowing him have told himself not to get caught again. He thought that I was just a stupid woman, well maybe in lots of ways I was, but I wasn't that stupid, that I didn't know that he was with other women. He would come home after apparently been in work expect his meal that was always ready and his clothes washed and the kids usually in bed. Then when we went to bed he would try to do whatever his latest girlfriend liked to do in bed with me and when I'd ask him what he was doing or as to why then he would freak at me. The look in his eyes to start with was scary, but at the end of my life with him it would terrify me. The rapes didn't really start here though he would make me or convince me that I would want to have sex with him. But he would be in control and he would be the one who said and did all, I was simply his puppet. Then there was a change in him he got more abusive, more aggressive, and edgy. To say that we all walked on eggshells is an understatement, anything and everything would set him off, we were a normal family when he wasn't there laughing, joking, arguing but when he would walk in the total atmosphere in the house would change and he could literally make us all shake with his glare.

It was 1997 and my third child had been born he was only a tiny little thing, he was premature and I know for a fact, that this was because of the stress that I was under at the time. Yes I was pregnant but he was having a deep affair and one that lasted over 6 years that I know off, it was the one that would finally show me who and what he really was. My son that was born was an un-identical twin, but at just over three months into the pregnancy I lost the twin, there was no explanation from the hospital, just that it was one of those things. But they didn't know my life, they didn't know the stress and strains that we were under every second of every day, if they did they would have said that this was the reason for the miscarriage. My son when born was put straight into ICU and as I call the microwave or incubator. He was there for about ten days but pulled through, and was one of the easiest babies that I have ever had to mind. I would wake him up to make sure that he was okay he was that quiet.

Since I was now busy with three kids it meant that Bas had a lot more excuses and time on his hands to be with other women, and to be involved in lots of illegal activities. That with me now so brain washed at the time in my life, I didn't see or realize what was going on. He was always flashing the cash now, money was no object to him, yes he worked long hours but the figures still didn't add up. He was now spending at least one or two nights away from home every week. His excuse he got work that took him down the country, and like the dutiful wife I believed him. I would make him a flask, sandwiches and spare clothes, god I even felt sorry for him thinking that we were at home all warm and comfy and he was out working. When in actual fact he was in a hotel with his girlfriend, again another girl that he worked with. But this one was different, this one he kept very quiet and well hidden, he had been with her three years before I realized fully that he was up to his old tricks again. The hardest part of this affair was in knowing the depth of his deceit, the abuse to me escalated to an all-time high and never relented, but the worst bit was that I had fallen pregnant again by him. To been honest I cried and cried I couldn't handle another baby so soon after my last and knowing that he was out messing around. I was an emotional wreck. But after the initial tears and the fears, I got a grip and decided to just get on with it. That summer he sent me and the kids to Spain for six weeks, he was going to join us after two weeks there.

Now I see that he had it all planned, he must have had a great two weeks with no wife, no kids, nobody to ruin his affair. I still shiver at the thought of her and him in my house in my bed at the time, but I know that it happened whilst I was out of the way. When he did come down to Spain he spent nearly every minute on the mobile of course blaming work and his family, but it was his girlfriend Jilly who he was in constant contact with.

One day he was cleaning his BMW convertible that he loved to pose in, when under the seat I found a passport belonging to a girl called Jilly. He took it from me and said that it belonged to his brother who was separated at the time, and it was his new girlfriends, like the fool I was I swallowed the story, hook line and sinker. His verbal abuse was the worst part at this stage, he was so demanding, so much of a bully behind closed doors but to the outside world we were the happy little family. God if they only knew. He would call me names, slag me about my looks, my weight, tell me how useless I was as a woman and as a mam, criticize everything that I did. Anything that went wrong it was my fault, he could never do any wrong. I had one friend at this stage who lived close by, but I never ever told her i couldn't .How could I embarrass myself, how could I tell her that my life was a lie. I couldn't even admit all to myself, so there wasn't a hope in hell that I could admit it to anybody else. One night I woke up to my son who was just over a year old now crying, I went into his cot and as I bent over I got a fierce pain in my belly I cannot ever describe this pain, but it was the most horrific and gruesome pain I had ever had even worse than labor. When I got my breath and settled my son I went back into my bed, I told Bas that I thought that the baby had choked on the cord, he shrugged me off, told me that I was been stupid and to go asleep. I cried myself to sleep that night, I didn't know what was worse the pain, the fear that my baby was dead or the fact that Bas didn't give a dam about me or our baby. The next day I was in agony all day long, so that evening he was not happy that he had to come home early from work.

Then on my own I had to drive to my then GP and get checked. She was a very good doctor but extremely straight and she just looked at me and said that I need to go to the hospital, that she thought that the baby was dead. To hear those words is indescribable, these things happen to other people not me, not my family, but it was real, it was happening and it was a situation that I had no control over. I drove home in tears, when I went in and told him what the doctor said he freaked, as we were meant to be going to the evening party of the wedding for the couple who were moving into the house beside us. I will never forgive him for that. My parents came to mind the kids and we went to the hospital, they were expecting us as the doctor had called them in advance.

I was attending Mount Carmel Private Hospital and because it was a private hospital and it was a Friday night the tests that they could do were limited. They did a scan and no heart-beat, then they did a special blood test that determines if the baby is dead a week or more as there will be certain toxins in the body. I waited hours for the results still hoping they got it wrong, but they said that the test was fine. But I would have to stay in till the Monday, as if I hemorrhaged, I might not stop and that they couldn't do anything else until the Monday morning. Well he had plans, so I had to go home. I signed the waiver and went home knowing that the baby in my tummy was dead and that if I started to miscarry the baby over the weekend that I too could be dead. As for Bas well he went out that weekend as usual with Jilly, god forbid that he would disrupt his weekend for the death of his child.

CHAPTER 5 – MY DAUGHTER

On the following Monday I was brought back into the hospital by Baz, my parents minded the other children. Thank god I didn't hemorrhage over the week end, but now was the hard part the scan to see what was happening. I had the scan and was told that the baby was dead, there was no heartbeat. I could see my daughters image, but just silence no ta dum, ta dum from the scan speakers just a horrible deadly silence. The radiographer brought us out to a small room where I had to wait for the doctor to come into talk to me about the next step, I was hysterical yet numb these things don't happen it was like a nightmare, that I couldn't wake up from. But it was reality and it hit me hard, very hard ,but in some ways the loss of my daughter made me have an inner strength, that I didn't use for years but it is what has made me a survivor.

The doctor told me that they couldn't do a cesarean section, but they would try to induce labor. They were amazed that I hadn't miscarried, as they said that from the size of my baby she had been dead about 4 weeks. This made sense as a little over 4 weeks prior to this, I had flown to Chicago and had suffered horrific pains and headaches whilst there, but they were not like anything before so I just assumed it was a virus or from the long flight and the abuse from him on our way there and when in Chicago. Now I knew it was my little and only daughter dying, it is hard to live with at any cost, but to think that if id said something I might have saved her life. But I know in my heart that she only stayed with me for a short while, but in that short while her work was done, my very own guardian angel.

Later on that day I was hooked up to a drip and then started the real life heartache, the drugs were to encourage labor, but whether it was the loss of my baby that was causing the problems or it was the medication we never knew. But I had to be taken off the drip as my heart was not beating correctly and it was also very painful. For four long days and nights the nurses and doctors kept giving me medication to help me deliver my baby, at this stage I didn't know if it was a boy or girl, but I just wanted it out. Yet nothing was working.

There was an amazing little nun who worked at Mount Carmel Hospital her name was Sister Maura, she was only about 4ft high, but when she walked into your room it was like an aura was around her. She had something special, that something magical about her. She came in to talk to me and to see if I was okay, she actually gave me her rosary beads that she had since been ordained. She told me to tell my other children about the baby not to hide it as to hide it will cause more pain and hurt in the long run. Her words were simply that kids are resilient, they will always bounce back, no matter how bad a situation is and how right she was at the time.

Although now I don't think kids are resilient at all .When she left I got out of the bed and went to the nurse's station, I asked them for all the booklets that they had on what to do if you lose a baby. They advised me not to read them till after the birth, but no I wanted to read them now, for some unknown reason I just knew I had to. It was one of the best things that I ever did, as it let me know what to expect and more importantly what to do when she was born. On the Thursday Night about 9pm Bas left the hospital, there was still no sign of the baby and my doctor was running out of options as the longer the baby stayed in my womb the riskier it was for me, yet they couldn't remove the baby either, as that was a higher risk a real catch 22.

I was lying in the bed crying, listening to the Boyzone song No Matter What, it was the number 1 song in the charts that particular week, and I knew that no matter what, I would always remember my baby and include him or her in our lives. Suddenly I felt that I needed to go to the toilet, but when I went in I needed to push labor was starting and I was on my own. I pressed the panic button and the midwife came running into me, she had literally got me up onto the bed, when I delivered my tiny daughter still in the protective sac, when she burst it, I just started to cry. She handed me my little daughter. Bas and my doctor came running into the room, he flung his keys across the floor and I just sat there holding this minute perfectly formed little baby in my hand. She had the smallest little knees, bum cheeks, feet, fingers, I had ever seen. It was hard to believe that something so small was dead whilst been so perfect. She had bright blue eyes and you could see the four lobes of the brain, the doctor said that she could see nothing wrong physically, but a post mortem would be needed to find out the reason but it was my choice. I declined, my daughter had lived and died all within 22 weeks, I wasn't going to have her now cut up for my own satisfaction, no she was going to rest in peace. After all deep down I knew that her death was on the hands of her own dad, due to his abuse and the stress we lived with. Sister Maura then came in and asked me could she take my daughter, she wanted to clean her up and to bring her back to me in a crib. I agreed and when she came back my heart melted. She had made this amazing tiny white crib out of frilled paper and a box, it was so pretty but it was the thought and kindness that had gone into the making of it that meant more to me. She placed my daughter in the crib and told me that I could keep her with me till I felt ready to let her go, and that she would bring her back to me the next day.

Some hours later she took her for the night, I assume to the morgue. I didn't ask and she didn't say, but the next day Chelsea my daughter was returned to me and she stayed with me the entire day. As for Bas, well he told my parents that he was staying with me at the hospital, as the caring loving husband he should have been, when in fact he was off with his girlfriend. I had just given birth after a horrendous week to his dead daughter and I was devastated. He was off out having fun with his girl-friend sick is not the word to describe his actions. I don't think there is one that is in anyway printable. But things only got worse, as my daughter had been born she now had to be buried. I was in no state of mind to do anything, but Bas was apparently busy with work, busy with the kids that my parents had and more importantly busy with his girl-friend so he didn't have the time to arrange her funeral. The hospital did say that they could organize it, but it wouldn't have felt right if they did. She was my daughter and we wouldn't be able to give her anything in life that she would have had, so to organize her funeral was the least that we could do or should I say I could do.

So I gave Chelsea to Sister Maura and I went down to the phone box on the ward floor and rang Glasnevin Cemetery our local church and priest, between them all I arranged her funeral. The following day they let me out of the hospital and I'd really wanted to find something for Chelsea to wear, but she was tiny so it was going to be hard. Again with mam minding the kids, I went again alone to the shopping center and I remember as clear as day walking around there like a zombie just crying. You see on the speakers in the shop, they were playing the Boyzone song which the kids and I renamed Chelsea's song. The words for some reason struck me hard and really hit home, the fact that no matter what happened in life I had a daughter and I was going to be proud of her. So I bought a little baby doll outfit, it was even too big for her, on the way out of the shop there was a stall that was selling name plaques with the meaning of names. I went over and gave my beautiful daughters name to the man working there, when he put it into the computer what came up made me cry. You see I hadn't told him that she had died, just her name and date of birth, yet her name meant Angel, it was so poignant I broke down. When I told the man why, he was gob-smacked. To this day that same plaque is hanging over my bed and it will always stay with me, no matter where I am in the world.

At the funeral the priest allowed us to play what was now her song and I carried her little coffin into the church, and held it on my lap till the funeral was over, we then buried her in Glasnevin Cemetery, in a plot for her and eleven other babies. We used to say that it was Chelsea's garden and when you would go to the graveyard although it was a sad and cold place to be, when you would walk to the angels plot there was a magical mischievous feeling to it, with all the wind chimes in the trees and the toys, teddies it was as if you could imagine all the little angels running around playing with each other and having fun. It was a place of pure peace and pure love the feeling that was there had to be felt it was not something that you could explain to people. It was one of those places where you just wanted to stay longer and longer, not a place of sadness but of cheeky little boys and girls all friends and the guardian angels to us all.

For years this was our only place to go to that I really felt close to my daughter, yes I knew that she was with me, I am a firm believer in the spiritual world not of any particular religion, but there are angels and spirits in my opinion. From what I have experienced personally in life, I know that they are there to help us through everything and anything that we ask them to help us with. But all of this was been taken away from not only my daughter, but from all the parents and families of children buried in Glasnevin Cemetery.

Bas had shown me what he thought of his daughter which was that she meant little or nothing to him. She was not important to him, in actual fact he sent me a text some years after her death to say that she was lucky that she hadn't lived, as she was better off dead than having a mam like me. Now as hard as that is to hear, especially from the dad of my daughter it just showed me what a low life and piece of scum he was and always will be. But his actions not only at Chelsea's birth, but afterwards with her funeral and then when she and her angel friends lost their resting place, it was one thing that I swore I'd never forgive him for and I never will.

The management of Glasnevin Cemetery had decided that they would get rid of all the individual headstones, the toys, the books. Literally anything and everything which made our babys graves special and personal to us all was to be removed forever more. They would in place of this make it into a rose garden for tourist's they would be walking on my daughters and all the other angels graves. It was like she was dying again, the only place that we had to go to see her or to be near her was the grave, yes there were other babies in the plot with her. But her little toys, her name plaque, her angel statues, they meant that she was real, that she was a little person. And that to me she, like all the others had a right to rest in peace, not to be a tourist attraction for the cemetery to make money off, a simple commodity in life.

So I started a campaign and worked 24 hours a day 7 days a week
It got lots of media publicity and people ringing me day and night with their stories, their heartaches and their determination to help stop the desecration of our babies and children's graves. Some of the children had two burials, as they had unknown to their families had their organs taken at autopsy and kept for medical science, until discovered and then either buried beside the baby or as close as possible. This angels plot meant so much too so many people.

Many of us were unable to get birth or death certs for our children
Yet they were real, they were human, they were born and either died or where stillborn, but to say that they didn't deserve a birth or death cert due to the age of the baby at delivery was bad enough. Now their final resting place, a place of peace and tranquility was been made into a tourist site. We discovered so much that had been hidden, so much about graves that should not be in the babies plots, and the more we discovered the more hassle I personally got. One Saturday afternoon I was at my late dad's house and I got a phone call from an anonymous woman, who was screaming and shouting at me. I had no idea as to who she was or to why she was so irate and upset. She continued to tell me that one of the persons who was involved in a prominent way in the Campaign, was her father and that he not only abused her for years, but also the baby that was buried in the angels plot in Glasnevin, the one that we were trying to save.

I was shocked and didn't know what to believe, however the details that she told me could not have been made up, they couldn't have been lies. She was too upset, too detailed and to in-sensed at the fact that this man who she claimed was a pedophile was involved with trying to save children. Personally I could fully understand her upset, I mean who wouldn't be. I contacted a number of prominent people in the campaign and told them including a Garda, who was also part of the campaign for personal reasons what I had been told. I was told that I should back away from this person and to try to get the campaign away from their grips. As everything and anything to do with him, that was associated with him, or the campaign and all our hard work would have been for nothing if this information leaked to the media.

Personally I got a lot of stick over it. So many people took their anger out on me. Then the death threats started to come and then Bas decided that he was the only one to abuse me and he stopped me and the campaign in its tracks. The Garda in the campaign heard him one night over the cell, he was verbally abusive to her and me, threatening and ensuring that I was so embarrassed that I wouldn't want to be seen near the campaign or certain people again.

The threat and danger to me was now not only from an outsider but from Bas, he wasn't the center of attention for those weeks and he didn't like it. He decided that everybody who would phone me that he would grab the phone first, or from my hand and tell them to fuck off, that the campaign was over. He didn't care that our daughter was there or that thousands of other babies were there no he wanted control back of me and he was going to get it one way or another. I didn't have a choice, I had to back out of the campaign, I couldn't tell those that mattered to me about my abuse. They probably wouldn't have believed me, as I covered it so well and even if they did what could they do. I had to stop fighting for the babies so not only had he caused as far as I was concerned with his affairs and abuse the loss of my daughter initially, he now had taken away the only place that I had to go to feel close to her ,what was her final resting place. I felt so guilty that I let so many people down, so many babies and for what so that I could simply live. This devastated me for a long time and to be honest, I am still not over it I don't think I ever will. But I know that at the time, I did what I had to in order to be alive for my other children and they were what mattered now, not me, not my daughter who I couldn't help just them.

Since that day I have not set foot inside the cemetery, in actual fact I find it hard to go into any cemetery even to visit my parents graves, it just brings too much back to me. The only way that I could keep my daughter with me, was in my heart and on me, so I got a beautiful tattoo of an angel. She is looking into a mirror as if she is looking at me and watching me, it is the first thing I see every morning and the last thing I see every night. She is my angel and she is and will be with me forever, I know I did my best to try to save her garden and that of her angel friends, but I just wasn't strong enough to chance losing my life, as then I would be no good to her or my other children.

CHAPTER 6 – THE KILLER AFFAIR

This was probably one of the hardest things that I had to deal with in this relationship with Bas. To have a secret life with another woman, with her family, to make plans for their future, to lie to his children, his wife his extended family and friends for this length of time beggars belief. However it also makes me wonder how many of these so called family members and friends knew what was going on, as from all accounts they were wining and dining in public and they once again worked together.

He even introduced some of my kids to her one day, when she was at the gym where he trained and thinking that they were too young to realize or remember said well this is your new mammy. Little did he know that one in particular remembered every word and every action that man took in our lives. She was a good looking girl in her early 20s, not married and only involved with him. As much as I blame her and hate her for her part of the affair, I don't blame her like I do him for the hurt and the pain caused. As she wasn't the one who was married, he was and she wasn't the one lying he was. I know all too well what a manipulator he is and was and she had truly fallen for him, she was in love and I think that he in his own way was with her. But he wanted his cake and the icing on it too. How powerful he must have felt to have a wife at home who he Controlled, that was his built in babysitter and a girlfriend who he worked with and saw all the time and who idolized him. He played both of us but in different ways. When I look back on this period of my life, I realized that I had given birth to one child in 1997, then buried my daughter in 1998, given birth again to my son in 2001, and lost his twin at the same time all whilst he was off playing with his girlfriend.

All the scans, the doctor appointments, the funeral for my baby girl all that I had to do alone, he did nothing, he was the man in the house and he could do as he pleased. I first found out about her the day before my son was born in 2001. I know it is hard to believe that for years he had been having an affair and I didn't know. I didn't ask questions as I knew not to ask, not to query and not to kick up a fuss. His violence at this stage was relatively still in its infancy so although I knew that he had a violent temper and would hit me, I did not know the extent of this temper or to the extent as to what he would do with it .I was in bed on the morning of 23rd July 2001 knowing that I would be going into hospital the next morning to be induced. The baby would be premature however he at this stage had a better chance outside of my body than he did in, as he wasn't growing and I had already lost his twin brother Michael some months earlier so he was at risk. The sad thing about the death of Michael was that it happened one hour after my late mam in law died, she died holding my hand and I was always very close to her. But she had lived a life of abuse from her husband, not as bad as her son but still enough to destroy part of her.

My reasoning for the loss of Michael was that Angel didn't want to go alone, so she took one baby, but left me with one so that was how I dealt with his loss. I know she is minding him in heaven along with Chelsea. Whilst in bed the doorbell rang and he went down to answer it, it was a friend of his and he brought him in. I stayed in bed as I was exhausted and really didn't want to go downstairs at that time in the morning, lucky for me I didn't. His mobile phone was beside the bed and I would not have noticed had it not bleeped with a message. Not knowing what he was up to, I opened the message and subsequently a can of worms that would cause massive destruction to a lot of people .It was a text thanking him for the night before with a kiss and love from Jilly, well I freaked I text him and told him and he came running up the stairs in a state of panic.

He tried to tell me that it was just a girl that he had helped in work, that was in need of a lift, I was pregnant not stupid, my brain did work and I knew there and then that he had been caught out. It was not the state that id wanted to be in at that time, especially with the birth imminent, I freaked for the day and cried more tears than a river. I rang her number but she said that it was a wrong number .I knew dam well that it wasn't, but right there and then I wasn't in the right frame of mind or had the strength to deal with it. My only worry was my little baby birth the next day.

The following day my parents minded the kids for me and we headed over to Mount Carmel Hospital where I was been treated. I started the medication within a short period of time for the labor to be induced. I was given the option again to hold off on the birth but either way was risky, and at least if the baby was out then we could ensure it got the medical attention it needed were as in the womb I couldn't watch or mind it 24 hours a day. I literally was waiting for something to happen and I wasn't going through the burial of another child. No they would induce me and that was that. It was hard enough that they had told me at just 20 weeks pregnant that at any stage I could go into labor and that at 28 weeks, I had to start to inject myself everyday into my belly with Dexometazone, which is a steroid to help strengthen the lungs of a premature baby.

Every day I wondered if today was the day that he would be born, I was petrified that id lose him. Hours passed before anything started but then it did, I was doing the usual walking the corridors hoping gravity would help but it was going to be a long day. I should have known it was a boy as already he was been awkward. While walking the corridors Bas was forever on the mobile if he wasn't answering calls or ringing somebody or texting he was gone outside for fresh air. I found out later that he received 35 phone calls alone from Jilly while I was in labor and he made the equivalent if not more back.

As for text messages I lost count after 50, so it was clear he was still lying and so was she. I didn't know which was more painful the labor pains that were coming on or the fact that the man with me was more interested in his mistress than his wife and child I still to this day cannot get my head around that but it shows how heartless he really was. After an entire day of labor and still very little happening, the doctors told me that if within the next hour I hadn't started to dilate fully that they would have to do a c section, as the baby's heart beat was slowing down and he was in distress. A section was the last thing that id wanted I was terrified and alone as Bas was more interested in his phone than me or the agony I was in. However literally 5 minutes before the hour was up I dilated fully I took it as a sign from my son's twin that should have still been with him, after a short labor my son was born.

But I could hardly look at him, I thought that he was dead and I just was somehow unable to believe that he was alive. He didn't cry or whimper and he was the snowiest of whites I had ever seen in my life. There was no color in his body let alone his face. Thankfully after a few moments he let out a big scream and he was put into the microwave as I call it, but the incubator and was brought to special care as he was very small and had hypothermia from the long labor. Then it went blurred, I remember the nurse saying her lips are gone blue and she is hemorrhaging than black, apparently I went into shock after his birth and passed a huge clot even though the afterbirth had already been passed. My blood pressure dropped drastically and they thought that I would die. I remember the before part and the after part but not the actual time that I blacked out. I was given blood and brought to my room. When we went outside the theatre my parents were standing there, but I couldn't talk to them. I just couldn't face anybody, yes id just had my son but in the space of 24 hours id gone from knowing my husband a bully, and violent man was having another affair, that he was a liar, and that he loved the girlfriend more than me. He told me that he was going to go home to my parent home and to stay there for the night. However he I assume thought that I wouldn't find out, but he never arrived at their house. Instead he rang them and told them that he would be staying with his friend as it was nearer to the hospital, so that he could be up first thing the next morning to me a lie again. No he spent the night with Jilly.

Clearly seeing me nearly die and his son been in the ICU ward still wasn't important enough to him for him to stay with me, or to go and see his other children, no having sex with Jilly was his priority and off he went. He didn't even arrive up to the hospital until after tea the following day, I was more interested in my sons health than him right then and something had happened inside me, something that had made me question my entire life with him. What I was going to do with the answers id no idea but I

40

was going to try and find the strength, somewhere, somehow to survive and to leave, sadly thinking this is one thing acting it out is another and it took many years before I had the strength and the mind power to stand up to him and to say NO MORE.

That was the hardest thing to do so far but was one of the best feelings ever. I took my power and my life back and now I would live it. At the time of his affair we were both with Vodafone and his account was online with mine so I became a detective. I searched through the bills found the numbers been called all day and in particular late at night or during the night and the text messages the paper-trail was unreal. I knew her name was Jilly but I didn't know anything else about her. Where she lived was I walking past her everyday did I know her, did she know me the mental torture was horrendous, so one night I went to bed and cried myself to sleep again. In my dreams I asked my daughter to let me know where she worked now I am not religious and didn't even know if it would work but I hoped that it would as I had no other way to find her. The next morning I woke up with a phone number in my head I couldn't get it out ,it was like a record that was replaying constantly over and over and I knew the number but couldn't figure out from where or how. Then it dawned on me it was the main switch number for his place of work again he had struck at work. I knew all his colleagues so they must have thought that I was a total fool to not have realized what was happening, but I was just naïve and brain-washed. So with him gone to work and the kids in school I decided to ring the number and ask to speak to Jilly.

Now I'd no idea as to what department she was in or if there were more than one Jilly's there but I tried. I didn't give my correct name as I didn't want to for warn her, and there was only one Jilly in the company and I was put through to her phone. God when I think of it now, that was one of the hardest things to do. Imagine having to ring the woman that my husband was sleeping with behind my back to this day. I have no idea as to how I did it but I did. I had to and I am not sure who was more surprised, but I did ask so should not have been so surprised that she was such a bitch on the phone to me. She was so cocky confident and arrogant, that really all id wanted to do was to reach down the line and punch her, but as much satisfaction that would give me she would have had the last laugh. They both would have as they would have charged me.

After sometime she hung up on me, seems like I hit a few home truth. But then Bas rings me he was freaking that Id rang her. I was the victim but he was worried about her, that in itself said more than any words he ever could. Apparently she told him to ring me or she would suppose he was afraid of losing her more than his family, as it turned out that not only had he bought her a red sports car, but he also was down with her family the previous Christmas on the St Stephens day. A day when he told me and the kids that he had to work .The only work he was doing was sleeping with the enemy and lying through his teeth. I decided to write a letter to the Managing Director of the company and tell him about the affair, I knew that there was little that they could do about it but at least he knew that when she was meant to be working for him and been paid to work for him she was on her mobile texting or talking to Bas. So inadvertently it was affecting his business. The funny thing was that this letter was opened accidentally on purpose by the receptionist at the company and the news spread like wildfire the entire company knew about them and they were both mortified. It didn't stop them just embarrassed them, but it was something at least. For a few weeks he seemed to be home from work early and there at weekends, so I was starting to think that it was over. But I didn't know at this stage that the affair had been going on for years. I stupidly thought maybe a few months, but I soon learned otherwise and then the vengeful wife decided enough was enough. Birthdays were always very special to me, you have to have a cake and presents, it doesn't matter what was spent on them, just to have them and a card is very important. I would always make a point of ensuring that all in our family celebrated in the best way possible.

Well it was his birthday in the November this particular birthday was on a Friday which we thought was great as we could do something, than nobody up early the next morning ,but he had his own plans. He told us that he had to go work down the country. Now he drove oil tankers so when down the country, his phone wouldn't always be in cover, so it was the perfect excuse for him. I felt so sorry for him made him a packed lunch/dinner clean clothes the lot and the bastard was laughing at me inside. Up until about 10pm that night he was contactable then the phone would ring and ring no answer it stayed like that until 2pm the following day. No texts returned no calls returned, just nothing. I didn't know right then whether he had been in an accident or was lying dead somewhere, or if off with his mistress. When he came back the next day he was all apologizes, the usual the battery dead but if battery dead you don't get a ring tone when you ring that number, so I knew he was lying.

He also had tell- tale signs of when he was up to his tricks. He suffered from a skin disorder well two actually one called Folliculitis and the other Rosacea. I was able to learn when he was up to his tricks just by his skin. If it was all red on his face and had little watery blisters then he was messing about if his face clear he was ok. I never told him that this was a sign, why the hell should I. We decided to bring the kids to the zoo as they had wanted to do something with him for his birthday. I went into the home office to empty the lunch bag and flask id given him, but when I put my hand into the bag pocket a receipt for a hotel fell out in his name and for the night before .As fuming as I was, the detective in me decided to play him now. So I rang the hotel it was the Deerpark Hotel in Howth Co Dublin. A good choice as a long way from our home, but also it is located in a secluded area, so unless you are staying in the hotel or from that area you are not going to go there. So their rendezvous would be safe. Anyway I told the hotel reception that id stayed there the night before I gave his name and hers. I knew it was Jilly again it just had to be and that I needed a copy of the invoice for my work expenses. They faxed it to me so there and then I had the confirmation that on his birthday he wasn't with his family, he had been off with his mistress, celebrating with room service and a bottle of champagne. I felt sick to the stomach, I had been fooled again. So I went into the kitchen and asked him about the card that I found, I didn't tell him about the invoice at this stage. No I was going to get him this time.

He proceeded to tell me that the card wasn't his, that as bad as it Looked, it actually belonged to one of his brothers. Now this brother was separated at the time and had the same initial. He told me that he had lent him his car as he knew he would be away working and that it must have fallen off the seat into his bag that I had packed. The details of his explanation were unreal and although I was listening and pretending to swallow it all. Inside I knew it was just another load of bullshit, but I couldn't wait to see his face when I showed him the invoice that was so going to be worth it.

After sometime of his crap lies, I decided to show him the invoice, he literally went white in the face, he drained of color and with what was his dark complexion or was should I say, he was caught hook line and sinker. Yet he tried to explain and tried to bullshit me. I knew that day that I no longer loved him, actually now I realize that I never loved him. I was just fooled and brainwashed by him, hindsight is an amazing thing, but you cannot change the past, but you sure as hell can ensure that your past is not your future.

He ripped up the invoice, but id copied it, I may be a woman but I am not stupid despite what he thinks. I threw him out, I didn't know what to do, he just went crazy screaming, shouting then flew off in his BMW no doubt to his Jilly. I was pacing the house. I had young kids a very young baby .I was in bits, where do I go, who can I tell? It was too embarrassing to tell people that my life was a total lie. He put on such a good show that nobody would believe me .After all what does a man who has affairs or abuses his family look like.

People that are ignorant will try to stereotype them into looking rough or from poor area or bad parents or tattoos, piercings. No the ones that you need to watch, are the ones that look like they have it all. The perfect life, the perfect family, the perfect front, these are the worst type, as they get to hide for many years sometimes a life time totally hidden behind this cloak of secrecy. We split up for a while and I tried to stay strong for the kids, I hated the thought that he was still with her or that he wasn't going to be around. As much as I hated him and his abuse, I was used to it that sounds crazy, but you become accustomed to your life a certain way and that was what had happened me. He didn't contact me for days, as if I was in the wrong, then he told me that he was staying in a flat, that a friend of his owned that wasn't been used. So he was going to stay there for now. I hadn't been in contact with her, but I had found her family address and their phone number. It was in another small rural town, a bit away from where I lived, but with motorways not that far. I rang her home and told her dad who answered the phone what she had been up to with Bas.

Now he screamed at me down the phone and hung up but it must have hit home, as she was told to leave their home and she unknown to me then fled to America, to stay with an uncle there for a while. So that she would be away from Bas and the entire situation. I know that she was an adult and that it wasn't her parents fault, but at least if they knew about them, then they wouldn't welcome him into their home, this is what I had hoped and they didn't .This friend and Bas association with him is another chapter but he was not a nice person, again he would be the mannerly gentleman that nobody would suspect of anything. I have no idea as to whether he was involved in a violent way with his wife, but I do know that he was involved with a lot of unsavory people. Along with Bas they were involved in lots of scams, this again I found out later. A few weeks after he left he arrived at the house and put a key onto a shelf in an envelope. I didn't know that he had done this, but for some reason he was been really nice and seemed genuinely sorry for all that he had done. He then told me that he was going away the next day for a few days to clear his head. That I wasn't to worry about anything that he had left something in the house for me and that he would call me in the morning and tell me where it was. So he said goodbye to kids and me and went. The next day I got a call from him on his cell, it was about lunchtime he said very little other than where he had left the envelope. He wouldn't tell me where he was going. However just as he was on the phone, I heard an announcement on a speaker in the background and I knew that he was at Dublin Airport. He hung up when I said that I knew where he was. I got down to work there and then, he had left me the key and address for his flat and had left a note asking me to clean it, of all the bloody nerve, but at least I had the key and I knew where I would be going. He didn't figure on me using my skills at what I used to work, at which was as a travel agent to track him down. I knew that the Doctor who had helped us escape from Bulgaria all those years before, lived and worked in Chicago and I knew that there was a flight there at about lunchtime so I added two and two and came up with four.

I then proceeded to ring the doctor in Chicago and gave him a bull
Shit story about forgetting the hotel name that Bas had booked into when he arrived. He very kindly gave me the name of the hotel its number and also his flight arrival. I got him and he didn't even know it, although what I was going to do with what I had found out id no
idea. Due to time difference, it was some hours before I could call the hotel .But when I did, I asked to be put through to the room for Bas and Jilly and guess what they did. They put me through to the voicemail as apparently they were out having a meal well I left them a voicemail that would probably have to have bleep, bleep, bleep for lines if I was to write down what I said. Boy did I let them know what I knew.

Then I got back onto the reception at the hotel, and with his credit card that I had all the details of, and knowing how he likes his champagne, I ordered a bottle of champagne to be delivered to their room with of course a lovely note attached. I very simply said that I hoped you enjoy your trip and get change out of your USD10 Bas, have a nice day love your wife and kids. God how id loved to have seen their faces when that was found in the room, and better still he paid for it, nothing like been a bitch for a day.

I then decided to ring her mam and to ask her what was going on that I thought she had thrown her out. She told me that sometime a go that Jilly had decided to go to the United States to her uncle who lived and worked there, he had his own business. As she needed to get away from Ireland and Bas, she couldn't handle not been with him, as she was in love with him. Her mam was furious even more so than me. She gave me the number for Jilly's uncle in Atlanta and I rang it, when I asked to speak to her, I was told that she had gone to Chicago for the week to meet an old friend called Bas from Ireland.

Now that was the truth there and then. I rang Jilly's mam and told her, she was so upset and disappointed in her daughter, that I really felt sorry for her. As it wasn't her fault. You can do the best possible for your kids in life, but at the end of the day they do what they want irrespective of what we as parents would like them to do or who to be with. She was so distraught she even offered for me to give the kids, down to her and that she would mind them, whilst I flew out to Chicago. That must have been so hard for her, to even contemplate let alone offer, but she did. Sadly I just didn't have the money to get a flight, so I didn't take her up on her offer. Bas was cute though, when he met our friend's wife, he didn't have Jilly with him, he knew that she would freak. I rang and told the Doctors wife what had been going on and she freaked out, she went crazy at Bas, so much so that he cut his trip short by a few days and she went back to Atlanta.

When he returned he tried to tell me that he wanted to get pay back for her dumping him and on me for making her feel she had to get rid of him from her life, all in one swipe. He tried to convince me that when he arrived into Chicago, that he rang her and told her that the trip was off and that he didn't want to see her. He was trying to tell me that he left her alone in Chicago, the problem with that was, that they both checked into the Best Western Hotel in the same room. So if she wasn't there, how did she sign the register and give her passport in as ID, the fact was they were caught out and they didn't know what to do.

A few days after he got back, I tried to ring her in Atlanta at her uncles plumbing business, where she was working. However she kept hanging up. So I sent faxes to the office with all the details on it and asking her very simply for answers to my questions and the simple question as to WHY. I got emails and faxes back and to this day I still have them, in them she apologizes profusely for all that they did. She tried to cover up a lot by saying she couldn't remember, but she just didn't know how to tell me .At this point I had actually written to her parents and told them what their affair had done to our lives, what destruction and upset that it had caused. But that I didn't blame her as much as him for the period before they knew that I had rumbled them. However since they both found out that I knew all them, she should have then walked, instead she stayed for more. That was what infuriated me more than anything, it was like double whammy.

Her mam rang me and we had along long talk I really felt so genuinely heartbroken for her, she was so embarrassed, but she had told her daughter, and her husband also had told her, that if she wanted to be with Bas, then she would be disowned by the entire family. They were cutting all contact with her. But as much as I hated her and I still to this day don't like her, I know that she was young and naïve, the cash was been flashed and anything she wanted he got for her, he used her just as he did me, I wrote to her parents and asked them to forgive her for what she did and to not let him destroy their family, like they had destroyed ours. After sometime they reconciled.

Jilly got into huge trouble in work, as all there saw the faxes as well so the embarrassment that id felt, when I realized about his work place affair, and how it now had come back on her. Now she was the one embarrassed. I didn't feel bad or guilty, I felt content, that id caused them some pain, I know that two wrongs don't make a right but it felt good at the time. The sad thing was that whilst they were away the kids and I went over to the flat that he had left his keys for, when we walked in it was in bits. But with Jilly in Atlanta and him meant to be living alone, he should have just had his stuff around the place. No instead he had a bundle of women magazines in the sitting-room and more tell- tale signs, the only bed in the flat had white sheets on it, with the pillow and sheets covered in false tan .I didn't cry, I laughed as he really just couldn't keep it in his trousers, of course he denied it, said that they were old stains. The problem was that he had bought them new in Penney's Dept store, so just more lies.

Jilly I truly believe that he loved, they had made so many plans for the future. Their future, not mine well mine included me not been there and me not been in my boys lives, this was when I first realized that Bas wanted me dead. They intended to move to Liverpool and to have kids, as his work had connections over there so they would be able to get jobs

there no problem. I have never found out for sure but I think that she had an abortion for him but I am not 100 % in this and suppose I never will be. She is the last id heard living in Australia she may very well be back in Ireland but hopefully she has realized what she and he did and that she never did get involved with another married man. Bas to this day resents me and hates me for causing them to split. He tells me in texts how she was the love of his life but she didn't know him, she saw the money flashing side, the fun side she didn't see the alcoholic, the
physically and mentally abusive excuse for a man who raped me no she saw his good side .But I am sure that if she had of stayed with him that she would be writing this book today not me, the evil in his eyes can never be shifted, as it is within him and that's what scares me the most.

CHAPTER 7 – THE DEVIL APPEARS

This chapter is one that has so much in it that it is hard to put it all
In too words and very hard to write .But I am not covering for him anymore or for who he was involved with. A lot of the following information. I can never ever prove they were always way too cute for evidence or a paper trail to be left but I lived with him. I know what he

was like and I know that he was involved in a lot of unsavory acts. As much as I would love to be able to prove all that I know about him, the one thing that I would love to be able to prove is how dangerous and manipulative a man he was and still is. I don't think that he will ever change, as for his entire life he has got away with so much that he thinks that he is invincible, so far he has been.

Bas has an arrogance about him that is impossible to explain but he has the look of pure evil in his eyes, this look no matter whether it's in a photo of him or in person literally terrifies me. It is one that cuts right through you, but it is a look that is full of evil and danger. I've only ever seen the same look in two peoples eyes, yet I have never met either of them and never want to. One of them is the scum Joe O Reilly, who murdered his poor wife Rachel so as to be with his girlfriend, he in so many ways was similar to Bas. On the outside he looked like the perfect gentleman, but behind closed doors only Rachel and her boys would have known the real devil that was Joe O Reilly.

There was also a man from Dundalk in Ireland called Michael McArdle. He threw his young wife Kelly Ann over a balcony when on holidays in Marbella in Spain some years ago. These two pieces of scum and that is the only word for them, are so similar to Bas that it terrifies me beyond believe .As like them he didn't and doesn't care about the effect the loss of a mother has on young children, no matter how much these men hated their wives and or their lives they could have just left.

But like Bas, it is a control issue, they have to be the ones to control everything in their lives and that includes whether or not their wives live or die, the kids well they are just really collateral damage.
As in time when they grow up they will if around these men, sadly be brain-washed into believing that they either didn't kill their mams or that they were driven to it. But either way they have won, as they have gotten rid of their problem as they saw it and even if in jail they will be released one day, when they will then live with who they want and where they want. Whatever woman is stupid enough to believe that their abuser won't hurt them, as he/she has changed is a fool. A leopard doesn't change his spots, they simply mask them for a while and history will repeat itself with an abuser as that is who they are inside, and no prison sentence will ever change that.

But I do not intend to be a statistic like poor Rachel or Kelly-Ann and if anything their loss and death, really made me realize how close I was to actually been them and been found dead. The thought of that is scary, but worse is the fact that I made children with this animal as did these women. We picked them from all the men in the world but we made bad choices not because we were stupid, no we made bad choices because they fooled us and brainwashed us from the moment they met us, and in doing so they managed to make us believe that they are simply great men. When underneath the exterior front, is a monster that is just teasing and grooming his prey.

Personally this is one of the hardest things that I have had to deal with is knowing that I was stupid enough to fall for him, that I was stupid enough to be brainwashed, and not listen to my gut or to other people .I would just think oh their jealous or they just don't know him, how wrong I was and how right they were. His violence was always there from day one but it escalated to a new level after we moved to his hometown and after Id found out about his killer affair. It was as if this was my punishment for disturbing his plans and his life after all who was I except his wife, built in babysitter, built in cleaner and built in punch-bag. In his eyes that was and who I am to this day, yet the day I stood up to him and took back my life is the day that I stopped been all of the above. It was this year that he would really freak at anything, talk about walking on eggshells this was like walking on cotton wool, no matter what I would say or do it was wrong and the punches would come.

One of the worst was a night I will never ever forget, it was one of the worst physical injuries that he gave me and to this day I still have that scar. I try to hide it with makeup and my hair sometimes it works and sometimes it doesn't. But to me every day when I wake up and look in the mirror, the first thing that I see is a reminder of him and of what he did, as sad as that makes me inside, it also makes me smile as I know that neither he or any other man will ever lay a hand on me again.

If anything the one thing that he can never ever take away from me, is my strength of mind and my determination to succeed and to have a happy life with my sons away from him and that is what I am doing. Our son was in the cot beside the bed on my side, as if he woke up at night I would just reach over to him and he would hold my hand and go back asleep, it was like a little comforter for him. Earlier that night Bas had been out as usual and came back in foul mood, so like the kids and I just went to bed anything to get away from him. As he walked into the bedroom I was in bed reading a magazine and he walked over to me. I cannot remember what he started shouting at me for or how the argument started, but I do remember the sudden pain that I felt in my eye. He punched me full force in the eye, I screamed with the pain and the shock and the kids came running in, he just walked out.

My eyebrow was busted open and bleeding even now I know that it should have been stitched, but I couldn't go to a hospital I wasn't risking losing the only thing that I had in this world my kids, they were my life and still are, even if some of our relationships are strained. My eye was so swollen that I literally looked like id been in a boxing fight, there was no way that make up would hide it, my eye itself was all blood shot and the rainbow in the sky didn't have as many colors as my eye and face did. So I told everybody that id been down at the Mater Hospital in Dublin the night before visiting my late mam who was suffering from Acute Myeloid Leukemia, and that on my way back to the car I was mugged, that I got hit in the face as I wouldn't give over my bag, it was a load of lies but what else could I do.

Bas seemed to enjoy the embarrassment and the pain that he caused me. In some sick way I think he actually got off on inflicting pain as he didn't just inflict it on me, he did it on lots of other people. He took steroids he thought that I didn't know about them but it was clear that he took something. He was big into the gym and weight training, but the muscles and strength that he got was only partly from training as he got so ripped and so big so fast that he had to be taking something. His moods were horrific, he would change in a second, one second laughing joking next freaking and smashing the place up. It was like living with a walking time bomb any second any word, any action would set him off and the consequences would always be horrific.

I lost count of the amount of plates and glasses that he threw on the Floor, sometimes they would be clean others they could have a dinner on them, or a drink in the glass. He didn't care he would cause the damage and then just walk out and leave me to clean up the mess. I would try not to let the kids see me cry or breakdown, but there was no point they saw his temper and heard him. Hell at times I am sure the entire town heard him screaming at me. His mental abuse was as bad if not worse at times then any physical or sexual abuse. As he would say things that he knew would hurt me, things that to this day still stick in my head.

Mainly how ugly I am, how fat I am, how useless I am, and how bad a mam I am. After years of been told this you do start to question if possibly what he is saying is the truth, deep down I knew that it wasn't. But I was starting to believe him, and at times thought that if I wasn't around that at least the kids would have a better life. If I was dead that as much as it would kill me literally in my heart to leave them. I knew they would have a better chance in life if they didn't have to grow up watching and hearing what he did to me.

Many times I will admit, I wanted to die it wasn't that I genuinely wanted to die, but more the fact that me as a person was already dead. I didn't recognize myself in anything that I said or did, no more than I recognized who he had become. It took a long time for me to realize that he hadn't become somebody different, he had just shown his true colors and who he truly was, the devil himself.

Id loose it after either he hit me or would have sex with me his way I would just lie there like a zombie, sometimes tears rolling down my face, as I didn't want him near me. But I knew that I couldn't stop him, in one swipe of his hands around my neck id be dead, so I let him do what he wanted to and pray in my head that it would be over soon. As soon as it was, I would grab the nearest thing to me whether it was a towel or a pair of my jammies as I didn't care, I would try to wipe myself clean off him. It didn't work, he was on my skin his smell would make me sick. To this day I cannot stand anybody putting their hands around my neck literally I just freeze up, even with jewelry. I just wear my Buddhist Mala Beads and they are the only thing that feels right around my neck, they never come off.

Most times after he would do the above I'd be found either by him or the kids sitting beside the toilet in the en-suite just shaking and hysterical, praying that I would die, praying that my life as I knew it would stop. It didn't it just got worse he enjoyed knowing how much he had broken my will in every way possible. One of the reasons as to why I never left was that other than the physical strength that he had I genuinely was afraid of him. I knew he had a lot of unsavory contacts and he also had an illegal gun in the house. He had it hidden under a loose floorboard that was at the entrance to our bedroom, unless you lifted the carpet you wouldn't have known what was under there. It was a 44 magnum handgun, and he knew only too well how to use it. He started to come home in the middle of the night in all different cars that I didn't recognize I probably would only see them once or twice, then never again. It is hard to believe that he could actually get more confident and dangerous than he was but he did. There was a new sense of cockiness about him as if he was thee man and nobody could ever touch him. The people that he was involved with I later found out where involved in the ringing of cars and laundering fuel from the North of Ireland and a lot more criminal activities. These were to include vigilantes against drug dealers. This point seemed hypocritical as many years later I found out that he was a dealer himself. Suppose it is a handy way to get rid of the competition.

He was for want of a better word partners in crime with two men that he worked closely with. One of them worked with him the other was involved in the same industry, however not directly linked to where Bas worked. They kept it tight only a few of them in their gang and that way nobody would be able to squeal or to cause them problems. If they did, they knew it had to be one of the three. They were involved in lots of things not that I could ever proof it they were and still are too clever to leave evidence around, but I know they were criminals of the worst kind. Bas always seemed to know a lot about certain crimes that would be reported in the papers or in the news. This wasn't just him bull-shitting he genuinely had details that were very real. From what I could see, what he would say was way too close to the crimes committed unless involved in some way.

He would arrive home some nights with huge big brown envelopes of cash, all used notes and would say that he had done nixer's or extra work and had been just storing the money in the envelope. What a gob shite I was, as I believed him. He had a safe in work and only him and his colleague knew about the contents of it. They weren't meant to have put their own locks on it for security reasons, but he did as inside that safe was a lot of money and at least one weapon.

It was the last place anybody would think to look, yet it was close to hand as he was always in or around his work place, if not for work then for one of the girls that was his mistress at the time. His friend who worked with him started to get a bit too flash for his liking, he was young, no commitments, no kids, just anything he got was for himself and he decided to flash the cash. He was I know known by the police as he was always been pulled in for something or other, but I don't think that he ever got caught. Maybe I am wrong and since then he has been caught and arrested, but somehow I very much doubt it, as they were very clever and had a tight crew. He was too cute for that, some of the cars that they were ringing would be stored in his garage, which was separate to his mams house where he was living in South Dublin, and therefor she knew nothing of what was going, on or if she did she turned a blind eye. Unlike Bas he wasn't violent to women, he actually would call down to our house after Bas would have gone on a rampage and either mashed the house or me up .But he would always try to help me clean up and or offer me money to make sure that the kids and me were okay.

I think that he was more taken by the money and the life in the fast lane with the adrenalin rush then been a criminal, but he was under the control of Bas and this other man who I will call Dave. Now Dave was violent and dangerous underneath the front he put on for the world, and behind his false life he was as bad as if not worse than Bas .He was the main one who got Bas involved with these people and this life he had as much control over Bas as Bas had over me and his friend Tommy at the time. Dave had his own fuel business and to this day he still has as far as Im aware.

He lives a good life, never short of money and always flying off to Puerto Banus in Spain, where he had an apartment and lived the highlife. I actually only ever met the man twice, and that was in Spain, however he was constantly in our lives organizing and planning whatever criminal act they were doing next. He was involved in the smuggling of fuel from the North of Ireland down to the south, but also in smuggling black oil which is a heavy commercial fuel up to the North. Bas would drive the tankers up sometimes his own tanker, other times that of Dave. In all the years that they were working together, they never once had the police near them, not for anything. They always said, well Bas always said that they had protection from a lot of people in the North and always implied that he was in the IRA .I don't think he was, in hindsight yes they had contacts, but they weren't as big a fish as they thought they were, they were simply wannabes.

When I started to ask questions and to realize what they were up to the level of violence escalated. I had to know where my place was. On one occasion I rang Dave and I told him that I was going to go to the police and tell them all that they were involved with and to finally shut them up. A stupid mistake that was, as they actually planned to bring me up to the Dublin Mountains and to gang rape me, to shut me up and to leave me there for dead if not already dead. As it would just look like a kidnapping that went wrong and then they were safe to continue their crimes. Apparently one night this was told to Bas and he must have found a conscience as he said that he wouldn't do it, so they beat the crap out of him, as a message to me. To be honest I didn't feel sorry for him, I just wanted out and if they murdered him, well then at least he was gone. I would only go to the funeral to ensure that the nails were fully in his coffin and only then could and would I be able to feel and live freely and not in fear. I still wait for that day, as they never took it to that level but when this book gets published then perhaps they will.

I really should have known all those years ago that he was really dangerous, there was one night when I was pregnant with our first son and we were in his family home. At the time I was living with his parents as there was too much arguing at my family home, re the fact that I was pregnant and not married. To my mam who would help so many unmarried mom's, and those in need to have her own daughter pregnant outside of marriage was a total insult to her. It was this behavior that made me really see how little I meant to her and that her love for me was not unconditional as it should be for all children especially from their mom. Angel who was Bas mam was very good to me and she took me in, and to me she was as close to a mom that I could want or ask for. We became very close.

This particular night we were watching the movie The Omen and I must have dozed off, but I woke with a startle and he was on top of me with a pillow over my face and his hands around my throat trying to strangle me, little did I know that this would happen so many more times in my life, thankfully he never succeeded. It was during this period that everything about him changed he started to become a monster. But a monster that could and would control his temper his mouth and his violence, only those that he wanted to live in fear of him would see him like this.

There was one incident that I think the kids and I will always remember, and it isn't a time or a situation that I am proud of, but there is no point in telling a story with only half truths. One night he had come home from work early he had that look, the look that just lets me know to stay quiet and or to stay out of his way. The kids would always be fed and either in bed or ready for bed when he would come in, as it was never early, but unusually he was home early this particular night. He was in a temper for god only knows what reason, I have lost track over the years, but he started on me the insults, the slagging, the imitating sexual actions that apparently I would be doing with all my lovers around the town.

He had made sure that I didn't have any life except my kids ,it wasn't worth the hassle going out, as I would always be afraid of him walking in the door of where I was or to him been told something that wasn't true. So the easiest solution was to stay at home, I knew someday when the kids were older that id manage to get a life, but for now staying alive and keeping the kids safe was priority However what I did next was one of the most selfish and stupid things that I ever did, but I was desperate, I genuinely couldn't take anymore of him or my life.

When his verbal abuse would get so bad that I could actually get away from him, I would go up to my bedroom close the door and go into the en-suite, I would sit in my little corner between the shower and the toilet and cry and cry, asking anybody that was listening why the hell had I to live like this. Nobody would believe me if I told them as he looked and acted the great dad, the great husband outside the house. This particular night he followed me up to the bathroom and started to kick the door in, as id locked it. I knew it was easier to just open it so I did. He started to drag me up from the ground but I wasn't going anywhere, then he stood there and kept telling me to die, just to go and die and how pathetic and useless I was. How he had to find a real woman for sex, as I was no good, and that was why he had affairs. I forced him into it, I made him be violent, as I was so mentally ill that I should be locked up in what was then Portrane Mental Hospital.

I was hysterical, I was shaking and even now many years later I can still see and feel the emotions that I had that evening. After sometime he left the bathroom and went downstairs to pretend to be the daddy that he should have been. I have no idea as to what came over me, but there and then I decided to end my life, I was too terrified to slash my wrists, so I got a bundle of belts and tied them together, I was going to throw myself over the balcony of the stairs in our house. I was sobbing knowing that id leave my boys, knowing that id no choice but to end my life physically. As inside my mind, I Lurleen had been dead for more years than id cared to remember. This was the final act. Just as I was about to get up onto the bannisters my oldest son came out of his room, I thought that he was downstairs, he started screaming at me to stop,

Of course Bas heard all the commotion and came running up the Stairs, true to form he stayed the bastard that I had grown to despise more than anybody else in this world. He didn't even try to talk me down or to calm me down, no he tried to push me up onto the bannisters, so that id hang, He actually wanted me to take my own life there and then in front of my kids and to help me do it. When I look back now on what I did I am mortified, but I can understand now my level of desperation. I didn't have anybody or anywhere to go, he assured of that, but then it hit me, if I died then my boys would be all alone with him.

I didn't think at that time that he would hurt them physically, yet I never thought that he could or would hurt me when I met him either so that scarred me, it woke me up, I was in a trance like state and eventually just took the belts off my neck and hugged my boys so tightly that I nearly squashed them to death. Id nearly done what he wanted but at my own hand, I would have died and he would have been the grieving widow and hero. That was something that I could not and would not allow to happen. This was one of the worst moments in my life, but it wasn't the only one where I had tried to end it all. As stupid as it sounds and seems to you, and I am the very first to tell anybody, that the first time that he strikes you is when you walk, In theory that is fine, but in reality with four kids ,no friends, very little family, no money, where do you go ,what do you do. As much as we were alone in this situation, we had a roof over our heads and the kids had some form of normality with school etc. So I decided to just stay and to stick it out, If I had have of known then that it would be another 10 years of pure hell, before we would get away from him, I wonder if I'd have still made the same decision to stay alive that evening.

But I am glad that I did, as now I have a life that I'm going to live and one that will be good instead of simply existing. Now I realize that I am a person, I am worth living and loving and hopefully someday I will find it, but for now I am happy been away from that monster and having my kids safe.

It was one of those years when everything was going wrong, I had just found out that two of my sons had a very unusual medical condition called Bilateral Micro- Lithiasis of the testes. It is basically pre cancer of the testes and extremely rare in Ireland. It is not a condition that is normally tested for, however one of the boys was always getting kidney infections, so when our GP sent him to Temple Street Children's Hospital for a scan they scanned the entire genital area and found just one week before Christmas, that he had this condition. There was no easy way for the radiographer to tell me, so she just said it out straight that my son had pre cancer of the testes. In over 20 years working at this hospital, she had not seen it in any child. However as it is not tested for in our hospitals it doesn't mean that other children don't have it. All that it means is that mine are the lucky ones, as they know that it is there.

As stupid as you may think it is that I say their lucky that they know they have pre cancer, the word Pre is the important one here. Since the hospitals here knew little or nothing about the condition. I contacted one of the best Children's hospitals in the world, The Cincinnati Children's Hospital in the USA, They were so helpful and emailed me details of tests that they should get done on a regular basis. So I went to the consultant and sat down with his team in the out patients clinic and told them all about Micro Lithiasis. It is basically calcium stones that can turn cancerous. There is no guarantee that they will turn malignant, however knowing that the condition is there is a bonus, as unlike most people who find out when it is at an advanced stage or perhaps when it is too late to do anything the boys know that they are regularly monitored. Every six months they get blood tests done called Alpha Feta Protein and Beta HGC Markers, these tests show if there is any change in the cancer level in their bodies, and if there is then they will get the medication that they require. So in some ways they are lucky as if it ever does turn, then it will have been caught early on rather than having been allowed to develop.

Even knowing this didn't stop Bas, he just passed it off, I am not even sure if he believed me or even with the medical documents. Honestly I think he thought it was all bullshit. As if living in an abusive environment and finding this out about two of the boys wasn't bad enough, it seemed that whoever had a voodoo doll out there with my family on it was back at work. One of the kids who was then only 8 years old, was out playing with his friends, nothing unusual about that. I cannot say which child it was but I got this feeling about 5 pm this particular day to ring him, and to ask him to come home on his bike. For some reason I was worried about him. Now nothing had warned me that there was something wrong, but I just had this gut feeling that all was not right. He didn't answer his mobile, but about ten minutes later he arrived home, he was white as if he had seen a ghost and very subdued, very quiet and very different. I asked him if all was ok and he said yes, that he was going to bed, this in itself was not normal for him so I was worried from the off.

Then I noticed that he was walking funny, his legs were not separating when he was walking, it was more of a shuffle than a walk and when he was getting changed, I noticed that his clothes were soiled, this was in no way him. Not even as a young child or baby had he ever had accidents so I really got worried. He couldn't sleep and wasn't eating now I know that the not eating was because it was too sore to go to the toilet. So if he didn't eat then the pain would ease. This went on for two days day and night, I knew that something had happened to him, I just didn't know what and id no evidence other than my son himself, so couldn't even go to the police. On the third day I managed to get him into a bath he maybe had pulled a muscle or something, as thinking anything else was just too much this was my baby my son, things like this don't happen in reality, its only in the movies how wrong I was. After an hour or two in the bath, were I kept talking to him , kept telling him that no matter what had happened or what anybody had said about him been in trouble if he told or that something would happen to his family, that he was safe that we were safe and that he just had to tell.

At this stage I actually thought that he had been raped by an adult, but what he told me was stomach churning and still is to this day. He had been up in his friend's house, the parents were out and there was a lady there as a babysitter, she was easily in her mid-forties and was a mam herself, from what I know. Anyway my son his friend and his friends brother, were playing pool in the house and having fun, my son went to take a shot and when he bent down his so called friend pulled down his tracksuit and boxers and stuck another pool cue up into his bottom. When he did this my son stood up with shock, and his coccyx was actually bruised in the process. They also perforated his bowel and that was what the soiling was from, as he couldn't control the leakage as the bowel itself was actually leaking feces.

Bas was like a mad man, storming around the house and it was one time that I did agree that I wanted to kill the kid, but I knew that we would end up then in the wrong. No this had to be done the proper way. I rang my GP and told her what had happened, Bas had to carry him out to the car, he lay face down in the front seat with the seat back on cushions as he couldn't sit down with the pain and every little bump was excruciating for him. He was crying and I was crying. I had to carry him into the doctors as he literally couldn't walk, my heart was broken, this was my son. Who would do something so sick, so evil, and worse why would they even consider it, or where did they see it. Our doctor who is still our doctor to this day, is amazing she actually started to cry when she saw my son and his injuries. He had the mark inside of his bottom of the top of a pool or snooker cue, you could clearly see the imprint it made. He couldn't sit down as the bruising on his coccyx was so bad that it was agony. She wrote me a letter and we headed straight for Temple Children's Hospital, where they were expecting us. I rang a social worker that I knew there at the time, as I had done some courses there on ADHD and had met her in the course of it. Also my son only wanted to speak to and to see female doctors.

She met us on arrival and the staff where amazing they examined him with such care, that I know they made it as easy on him as they possibly could, they x rayed him and told me that the perforation in his bowel had started to heal, as in a young child it would naturally start to repair itself after three days or so, and at this stage we were nearly into our fourth day. We were given painkillers and told him to rest. After speaking to the social worker and telling her what had happened, she told me that she would be contacting the HSE which was the standard course of action due to the circumstances. Id no problem with this as I wanted this child and his family to be held accountable for his actions. The following day we were given an appointment with a social worker in the local health board to discuss what had happened, the social worker said that he had no doubt in his mind that my son had been sexually assaulted and that he couldn't understand where another child of the same age had actually seen this action, or even thought to do it to another.

This was one of the most worrying aspects outside of my sons Welfare, as to me this was not normal, kids hit, they shout, they bitch but to do this to a friend was not normal and the fact that there was a little girl in the house scared me more. I was wondering is something happening to her or has it happened to others in the house, my mind was in overtime. We were given leaflets for counseling for our son in CARI which is the organization in Ireland for children at risk in Ireland. Although he wasn't at risk from us he had suffered a sexual assault, as an object had been inserted into his rectum by force. This in my eyes is rape no matter what the age of the perpetrator it is rape clear and simple. The local police came to the house, and took statements he was horrified, everybody that was involved was horrified, and I promised my son that by telling the truth that he would get justice for what was done to him, how wrong I was.

Within 24 hours of me been made aware of the assault, my son had gone to the doctor, been to the hospital, spoken to the hospital social worker, spoke to the HSE social worker and been referred for counseling for sexual assault, although there was a two year waiting list. Then he gave a statement to the police. The thug who assaulted my son was spoken to by the police after we made the complaint, however it was eight weeks before the HSE spoke to him that gave him plenty of time to get his story straight, and to rehearse his lies.

I wrote to the HSE so many times complaining about it, but there answer was well he is only 8 years old so we can't really do much, as they were both minors at the time. Despite the medical reports from the doctor, from the hospital and their own social worker they did nothing, they just filed it away it is a pity we couldn't just do that, and my son certainly couldn't. This thug was in his school, was in his class and I asked the principal to move this child, his answer was well if the police haven't charged him there is nothing that I can do, perhaps you should move your son.

Talk about getting rid of the victim. I contacted many times the Superintendent in the local district where we lived to ask him why the hell nothing had been done, that this was rape. If he had of been an adult and did the same to another adult there would have been charges of rape, so as a child why were they ignoring it. His answer to this day makes my blood boil, he told me that perhaps I need to get counseling, as clearly I have a problem as I can't let go of what happened. He is bloody well right, I will never get over my son been assaulted together with the fact that this child got away with it. If he was able to lie to get away with this at 8 years old, what the hell will he be like when he is an adult, I will tell you, he will be like my x Bas a total scumbag who thinks that he is invincible. To this day the fact that my son has never gotten justice it is sickening. Despite all his apparent connections and all his talk Bas was as usual no use, he would go to work, go to whatever slut he was with this time, and then off to his criminal life then at some stage he would come home. I was like a single parent, I was mammy and daddy all that he did was supply us with money, which later I found out was dirty money, but how was I to know. I was just told it was his wages that he had cashed his checks on his way home in the pub. I was such a fool. Some may think that I knew what he was up to, what the money was from, but I didn't and to this day I still don't know all that he did outside of the home.

I just know what we were subjected to and perhaps that is better as if I did know who and what he was doing in detail, I would probably be dead right now. Bas arrogance was endless, it was in this year that a friend of his died in an accident in Spain. He slipped off a boat whilst alone and banged his head off the side of the boat or the dock, however he died and it was a very sad time as he was just a normal guy unlike Bas and was not into the life that Bas was, he was a friend from another part of his life. When he found out that he had died he came home and went nuts, he walked into the kitchen and started to smash it up he threw pots, pans, plates, you name it they were just been flung left right and center, I told him that I wished it had of been him that died instead of his friend Lee, but that infuriated him even more the place was like a bombsite when he stormed out.

When the funeral came I was dreading it, as you would never know what he would say to you in front of people just to humiliate you, or to cause hassle that was him. He had now got so confident in his abuse having never been caught, that he didn't care if he embarrassed us it was all a big game to him. The funeral went ok and then onto the drinks in the pub and the food, this is normal at any Irish funeral, it is nearly like a celebration of their life. Anyway we had the kids with us and he was getting drunk as usual, he was drinking now all of the time, but when I asked to leave he would freak at me, he kept staring at this blonde over the bar and I knew that he knew her, but when I said it to him he freaked at me, I was mortified in front of everybody.

So I walked out with the kids and got into the car to go home, he stormed out after me and got into the car, the abuse was all the way home and all that night .How I regretted opening my mouth, I was now at one of the lowest points in my life. It turned out that the blonde was his latest conquest who was at the funeral and the pub as support for my then husband and worse he had asked her to come, how brazen can you get. She may well have thought that he was all that and more, but the real Bas she didn't know she saw the one with the flash car, the flash lifestyle and the happy go lucky guy who would buy her all she wanted and in return all he wanted was sex anytime, anyplace, anywhere and like a fool she went along like her predecessors, and obliged. I often wonder what they would have done if they saw or knew the real Bas, I am sure that they would have run like a bat out of hell at the first opportunity, I wish I had of but hindsight is an amazing thing, then again if I hadn't of lived the life I have, then I wouldn't be who I am today.

In some ways all the horrible things that have happened as much as I wish that they never did occur, they have made me mentally so strong and determined in my life, that I know I will find happiness and that I will not allow him to take another minute, let alone day of my life. He then tried to convince me that he was sorry, that he was going to do anything that I wanted, I could have anything in life that I asked for ,but inside I knew that I didn't love this man I never did. I was just a young teenager infatuated and stupidly I thought it was love. No my heart belonged to somebody else who I knew loved me and who I loved deeply, but I was married and so was he so nothing ever happened between us, but the connection was unreal and that was true love. The sad thing is he has since died I don't know where he is buried or even have a photo of him, but I know that he is with me. He is the one that has given me the inner strength to get free and to live my life.

I remember one night going to bed some years after his death and I had such a vivid dream of us just talking whilst having a cup of tea, but it was so clear and detailed it was as if he was sitting there with me. When I went asleep that night, I asked him in my head for a song that I could say was our song, something that would mean a lot to me and him. I also told him that I wished I had something that was his from over the years, just so that I could keep it with me. The next morning I woke up and I was singing a song, now I cannot in anyway sing, I am worse than a banshee, but I was only singing a few words of the song, and I knew that he had answered my question. I went out to the shops and searched for the song, eventually I found it and I listen to it non-stop when I'm having a bad day. The song was very significant in my life, it was by the band The Police and was called Every Breath You Take, the words say that with every breath, and every move I make that he will be watching over me and I know he is. I have been in supermarkets and just pottering around thinking maybe of him and the song just comes on over the speakers, it has freaked me out a bit at times, but I know that it is just to reassure me that I am not alone.

About a week after I got the song, I suddenly decided to clear out a few old boxes, but when I looked through them I found four old Christmas cards from years ago, all from my true love. There was no message just his name signed, but to this day I carry one of the cards folded up in my bra beside my heart, as this way he is where my heart is and I know that if I am having a bad moment or if I really need him that he is close enough to me to know. Stupid and rubbish I know some people will say, but I am not overly religious and it has helped me in life, so personally having the spirit of my true soul mate around me gives me security.

I also know that Michael and Chelsea are around me and always will be. We decided to buy a townhouse in Spain after all we spent weeks down there every year and the kids loved it ,also it would be my escape from him if we had to flee. We bought a three bed townhouse in Vista Azur in Estepona and when we weren't there we would rent it out. My very good friend Yolanda who lives in Spain, looked after the house for us and would ensure that there were no problems. Initially this all went well, until he started to go down to Spain a lot on his own, especially for long weekends. He knew Yolanda and I were extremely close so he wasn't going to show off anybody to her, as she would tell me but if he wasn't with other women, then why was he flying down and not answering calls.

Later I found out that the was actually having flings with women down in Estepona, as if doing it in Ireland wasn't bad enough now he was doing it in Spain, where lots of people in the area knew me and the kids, When I found out I was so infuriated that I honestly wanted to kill him, but I would never have the guts to do it, I just had to stick it out. Then he started to speak about living in Spain full time. His job driving the tankers was not bringing in the money like it used to do, a lot of the nixer's were stopped and the contracts that he had were been changed drastically at renewal so he suggested us moving to Spain for good.

I loved it down there, so yes I jumped at the chance a new life, a new start why not. Maybe it was just what we needed as he would have to be around me more and wouldn't be able to do all that he was doing in Ireland, god how wrong was I. Again he was back to going down at weekends, he went to a little fishing town called Sabinillas in Manilva, which is about ten minute drive from Estepona and only twenty minutes from Gibraltar. Which meant that we could get a lot of our foods in the supermarkets there like Sainsbury's, so it seemed as if we had it all sorted out, but I soon learned differently. He found lots of nice houses and villas but one in particular he fell in love with, it was a villa in Sabinillas and it needed a lot of work done to it, as it had been left in a neglected state, but the potential to have a mansion made out of it was very real.

He brought me down one of the weekends and we viewed the house, I initially wasn't a 100% sure about it, but he told me all that we could do and what he could do, so I agreed and we went ahead and bought the house with a mortgage. When the time came to move to Spain, our own house wasn't sold, so it was very hard financially to do the move but we did. I flew down with the four kids and dog and we had planned to move straight into the house, however when we arrived we were told that the owner was still in the house and that it would be at least a week, if not more before we could move in. Devastation and panic hit me, where would we go, we hadn't factored for this to happen and it was the height of peak season in Spain it was August.

Thankfully the estate agent got us a house to rent for the week so we had at least somewhere to stay. When the time came to move into the house, the boys and I had been there a week before Bas arrived. He was driving down from Ireland with the contents of our house in the truck. We decided that we would open some form of business in the town, as otherwise we would have nothing to live on, initially he wanted to open a gym, I am sure he just wanted to look and pick up all the women and the staff there. But after a lot of discussion, we decided to open a DVD store and a chocolate bar.

He went back to Ireland to work and was flying down to Spain every Friday or every second Friday and go back then on the Monday to work .Leaving me with four kids none of us spoke the language, all the paperwork for the schools, to be sorted, the shop building to be started it was a nightmare. In Spain if you rent a business in a new building the walls etc are only for cosmetic purposes, you have to put everything in from the wiring for electricity, to the pipes for water and toilets, to windows and doors and all this before you even buy a shelf. It is a crazy way that they do things. On top of this you need a license from the Ayuntamiento, which is the equivalent of our councils for every little thing that you do, and of course this costs money.

Eventually after a nightmare time with the builder that he hired who was not doing the work, who was robbing us blind as he knew that Bas wasn't there the shop was finished. It had cost us double our initial estimate as I had to get a new contractor in to fix all the first ones faults. Now the fun started, when the shop and chocolate bar was open it was going well, the only problem was that I didn't speak Spanish. So I hired a staff member who did, it was the logical thing to do. However as we sold beer and some spirits it was a great excuse for Bas to be having a drink, his excuse was that he was socializing and building up customers, all he was doing was drinking the profits.

His temper in Spain exceeded all his previous rages this was at a new level and this level he never reduced. He had by now quit Ireland and was living down with us full time, god how I wished that he had of just stayed in Ireland, as the kids and I would have had such a better life. Anyway he didn't, he came down to Spain. Our house had been sold at this time so he went out and bought a white Chrysler Voyager for the family. I didn't like it but he wanted to flash the cash, he paid Euro 25.000 for it and when I left Spain, I didn't even get Euro 10.000 back and this just went on paying the removals company and lawyers.

He would come home at all hours of the night drunk as a skunk, literally falling in the door. The kids would be asleep, but he wouldn't care. One night he came home really abusive and very drunk, he had tire marks what looked like from a bicycle or a motor bike on his back, and every time he got up off the floor, he would collapse back down onto it face first, if we went near him he would freak out and lash out at us. This was to become the new norm for us and I realized that no matter where in life we are, once he is in our life then we will just exist we would never be able to live. He was the one who controlled everything that happened or was said, no matter what we thought we were trapped for now anyway.

One particular night and I have no idea as to what set him off, it could be that somebody moved his bottle of gin or his can of beer whatever it was, I am sure of one thing it wasn't anything big or important it was just his trigger point and excuse to lash out .He started screaming and shouting, throwing plates at us, smashing the glass in the doors, so I put the kids into the car and we went to see there ponies at the equestrian center. I knew that it would keep us all occupied for hours and we wouldn't be thinking about him, at least for a while anyway.

A few hours later it was early evening we went home, from the outside the house was in darkness which was very unusual. My gut was telling me that there was something wrong, so I made the kids sit in the car, my now 18 year old insisted on coming in with me, he was the one who was never afraid or intimidated by Bas. Yet he was also the one who Bas picked on the most, the reason for that as far as I can see is that he couldn't control him or abuse him like he did me, so if he pushed the right buttons he would get the right answers and world war 3 would start.

When we approached the house there was a real evil feeling about it, I knew that there was evil waiting for us. We walked into the hall way and saw glass everywhere, the place had been thrashed, but all still in darkness. We turned on the lights and started to search for him .There he was in the sitting room with the microwave, I have no idea as to how many knives that he was holding, or that were around him. I think every knife in the house was there, well anyone with a blade sharp enough. He had put petrol into the microwave we found out at a later stage and his plan was to kill me, then to barricade himself into the house. He had recently had a new hall door made and had it fitted with a lock like one you would find in a castle, it was a chunk of 4 x 4 that slid across the back of the door and nothing would get past it. He also had a spy trap door in it so that you could talk to him, but not get at him. I used to think that this door was made to keep people out, now I know that it was made to keep people in mainly me.

He came at me and Jake my son that was with me with all the steak knives in his hand. We had to fight him off, he was like an adrenalin crazed lunatic, I had never seen such strength or determination in any bodies eyes he was going to kill me and he was going to do it there and then. Somehow he managed to get me separated from Jake and down into my other sons Marks bedroom, he had me up against the wall and actually had a steak knife and a fork in his hands, whilst holding me against the wall with his body, he was trying to stick them into my head. I was fighting him off by pushing them away. Jake managed to get back into me and he punched him hard, he wasn't expecting either him to come in or to be hit, so it dazed him for a second ,it was enough for us to get out and to open the door.

I have no idea as to how we got out of there that night, as he came running after us and actually chased me on the street whilst I was on the phone to the Guardia Civil, which is one of the police forces in Spain. They could hear all the screaming, I was hysterical, I had the kids in the car, and had got them to lock the doors. They were watching as I was been chased around the car by this psychopath with knives. I hung up the phone, I just knew that I had to get into that car, I screamed at Jake to open my door and as I ran around the next time I jumped into the seat and locked the doors, I flew off like a racecar driver.

At this moment I was in no state to drive, no state to do anything and certainly not to have four young kids with me, who at that moment in time where terrified that I was going to be murdered right in front of them. He didn't consider them, what my death would do to them, no more than he considered how upset that they would be watching what he had just done. He simply didn't care and to this day he still doesn't. I figured out then that he could not in any way have a conscience like most people would, this showed me how dangerous he really was.

I rang my dad back in Ireland and was hysterical on the phone, I have no idea as to why I rang him or as to what I expected him to do for me, after all we were thousands of miles away and so alone. Dad just kept telling me to come home and to tell the police, I did tell the police but by time they got up to the house to talk to him he had it all cleaned up and excuses for everything. This situation happened so many times in Spain that it is a miracle that not only I but that the kids as well got out alive. As much as Bas hates me and hated me, he thought that he owned me in his mind, he was far more concerned that if he couldn't have me then nobody else would, but been with him would turn you off men for life.

We would stay in a hotel / apartment complex that was near the house and wasn't expensive. So we could flee there in the car when we needed to escape, they started to recognize us at reception and I was worried then that they might report us, staying there as we always would arrive late at night. I was scared that I might lose the kids, so we stopped going there. On one occasion we were at the stables in Estepona, the Escuela Arte de Equestria, it was a great place the boys had bought themselves ponies out of my late mams inheritance. They were only cheap ponies, but they meant the world to them. It also meant that we had an escape from the house, we could go there and spend as long as we wanted with the horses and ponies and talk to them without fear. Qualqi-Jac and Simba were the boy's ponies and Marachina was the horse .One day there had been a very bad fire in the stables close to where the horses were and beside our tack room, it destroyed a lot of the building but thankfully the animals were ok. When we went up the next day to see what happened and to check on the horses, we were asked by management to move everything from the tack-room as they had to demolish it after the fire. Of course Bas was with us, well he was in the bar getting his gin and tonic and he then sauntered down to us drink in hand at 10 am in the morning.

He wasn't going to help, all he was doing was shouting at me as if it was my fault about the fire. Everybody was looking, it was totally humiliating and embarrassing for the boys and me. It is bad enough that he does this at home, but now he was doing it in public, the humiliation was unreal. I stormed out of the tack room, he screamed after me at one point and he told me to look around, when I did he threw a hammer at me, it missed me by inches. At this stage he had now crossed another line, as he didn't care if people saw him abuse me, he had that arrogance about him, that he was truly invincible, and for so many years he was. Sadly in some ways he still is today. Shortly after this happened, he once again went on the rampage at the house. Poor Jack who was only 4 at the time ended up getting a punch in the face from him as he swung at me or one of the others and hit him instead. That action itself would shake most men into reality, but no he went mad. He was like a wild animal that was on a mission to destroy all in its path.

Again I called the police and this time they came to the house, they asked him what was going on and he told them that he hated their country that he was going home to Ireland the next day. They said that this was a good idea. If not they would have to arrest him as the children had been there to witness the abuse. In Spain family is very important and children are sacred. So they do not tolerate any form of abuse towards them or near them. Next day he simply vanished he had a taxi pick him up and he went to the airport. He had left me with four kids, a business that was open 15 hours a day seven days a week, two ponies and one horse. All their lessons and school runs in between, but he didn't give a dam he was thinking of himself.

Of course he also took a lump sum from our bank account leaving me struggling. Life was hard before, but it was even harder now, as I didn't know where he was or if he would just arrive at the door. Not knowing is harder for me anyway to deal with, than knowing something, as if you know where somebody is or what there up to you can deal with it. But by not knowing your mind runs away with you and you are in a constant state of worry. So I snapped myself out of it and got on with it. We didn't hear from him for about a week, he was in Ireland in Galway and apparently at interviews for jobs. It was bull he was with his x, which one I don't know but I have an idea. It didn't matter as I knew that he was lying. He didn't care about us about how we were managing, he just said that I would be fine, and that he would be in touch soon.

We got into routines, yes life was very hard and very much a struggle but we did it and better still we did it alone. I think that fact nearly killed him, as he didn't expect us to survive how wrong he was .On one of his prior tantrums for want of a better word, when we were in the villa he had gone downstairs to the garage and had locked the doors from the inside .We figured he was drinking as usual, but when we were all in bed asleep my mobile rang and it was him. I couldn't understand what he was saying except the word help, I shouted for Jake and we ran down to the garage, we looked in the top window and saw him hanging from the gym unit. He had locked the door from the inside. I have no idea as to how Jake got that door open, but he did, and I held Bas legs as Jake cut him down .The bastard just hurled curses at us and laughed, this was a joke to him ,to have his son see him hanging, to have his own child have to cut him down, and then to laugh at him and me is totally sick.

What type of parent does that, in my eyes one that is very sick and evil to the core. There isn't a day that goes by where Jake and I don't regret leaving him hanging, if we had of just left him there, at least then we would have had our lives back many years ago. As sad and horrible as it is to wish somebody had died, when they are destroying so many lives and want to kill you, then it is a matter of survival. A few months after the above, the boys and me packed our bags and came back to Ireland, life was too hard on my own with very few friends that could help us, and with no break just constant work. The kids and I daily struggling for money even though I was working my ass off to pay the bills, life in general would swallow every cent I had. Also my dad at this stage had been diagnosed with Bowel Cancer and since my mam was dead, I wanted to be there to care for dad, he didn't have anybody else to look after him except his two sisters .But they had their own lives, it wasn't fair to impose on them and dads neighbor Anne, who basically adopted dad while I was away .Then when I came back she was my eyes and ears for him when I wasn't up at his house, to make sure that he was okay. There is nothing in this world that could ever be enough to repay her kindness to my dad and me.

CHAPTER 8 – LIFE BACK IN IRELAND

When we came back to Ireland the kids and I were really very Upset, we had loved Spain. Yes it was really hard and we had to learn to speak a new language. However the warmth, the relaxed nature of the people and the country that you eventually end up becoming part of, is hard to explain but is a wonderful feeling. Literally where anything that needs to be done will be done. Just not in any type of hurry, as in Spain, manana which means tomorrow sometimes takes a long time to come around. However in some ways it's good as you relax more.

We hadn't left Spain as the boys and me had failed, no we left Spain as we didn't have a choice, going home to Ireland wasn't going be much better. We were going back to nothing we literally had our possession's that was it, where we were going to put them was another story but something would work out it always did. We moved in with my dad initially. We didn't have anywhere else to go however in a way it also suited dad, as at the time it was company for him, he was still missing my late mam. Bas was looking for work and I was trying to get the kids settled back into some form of routine and normality. Work was hard to find, there was very little out there and what work was there was either paying so little that you couldn't support a family on it or the work that they expected for the wage was unrealistic. So for a long time he had to claim social welfare. This was to be his excuse for the next few years until he got work, as to why he drank so much and was so abusive.

It is hard for anybody to go from having no worries about money and living the high life to having absolutely nothing. But what Bas forgot was that it was not just him who had been affected by all of this it was the entire family especially the kids. They wouldn't ever ask me for anything, they didn't ask for money to go out or to get new clothes. Even though they were now at the age where they needed a lot more as they knew the pressure we were under. He was now dropping kids to school then would disappear to the beach he would say for a walk with the dogs .The funny thing was that when he came back, he always stank of cider and his eyes would be blood shot. I learnt to be careful what I would say to him when alone there, as I knew that if he went off on one of his tantrums as I called them, then I would be dead .There was no two ways about it and I wasn't going to have my kids come home from school to find me gone from their lives, it just was not going to happen, not then not ever.

As terrified as I was and I still am to this day, I have built up a resilience a determination to stay alive to insure that he doesn't get to me. That no matter how much fear I am in of him, I will do whatever I have to do in order to stay on this earth with my children. If the police in Ireland cannot protect us, then we will relocate to somewhere that can .As no matter what we are going to live our lives and we are going to all grow old whether Bas likes it or not.

On top of the dropping kids to school, he then started to go to a small pub in the middle of nowhere .This was about half way between the schools and our house that we were now renting in his old family town. So it was a handy stopping point for him. Anyway as is the norm in a lot of small rural pubs in Ireland, they didn't stop serving you alcohol, irrespective of the fact that they knew that you were driving or that you had kids to collect. No they were there to sell alcohol and whoever bought it didn't matter to them, as it simply wasn't their problem. So many times he would get the kids then I wouldn't see them for hours. The mobile wouldn't be answered and he would just send a text playing with kids on beach or playing pool he was trying to justify his behavior with doing things with the kids.

If he was on the beach I guarantee that he had his cans with him, he never went anywhere without cans or some form of alcohol. One particular evening he had brought three of the boys to the beach for a walk with the dogs or so he said ,hours passed and there was no sign of them no answer to the phone either .So I knew that he was gone to the pub with the boys .Now he was driving a commercial jeep at the time, so he shouldn't even have had them in the back but he did .As I was about to leave the house to go and get the kids from him in the pub and probably throw a pint over him, my mobile rang it was him the devil himself.

He told me that there had been an accident, I freaked at him I went ballistic, I didn't give a dam about him, but if anything had happened to my boys he was dead. I would be done for murder if he harmed them in anyway .He started his abuse, his usual insults and his name calling, simply whatever he could come up with in his drunken state. I got into the car and flew over to the site of the crash, Jake was freaking at Bas as not only was he drunk, but he had taken a bend that is notorious for accidents way too fast and lost it. The jeep went into a ditch. Poor Jack was in the back of the jeep, with no seat belt, no child seat nothing at all to keep him safe. He simply had a horse stable door guard that was across the back of the front two seats. Only for Jake putting his arm out to catch Jack he was gone thru the windscreen and he would have been killed .I thought well maybe he will kop the fuck on at this stage. But no, he had managed to get another drinking buddy to bring a tractor down to pull the jeep out and gave me the kids. I took them home and as for Bas, well Bas went back to the pub to finish drinking and to tell the tale.

He was proud of himself for some unknown reason, he stumbled into the house hours later .Totally pissed and what was worse he had driven that jeep again with twice as much drink on him, he never got caught, he never got a ticket or a fine, it was as if he was invisible to the police irrespective of how reckless he was. His drinking and driving was just another blatant way of trying to think that nobody would get him for anything that he ever did. And in some stupid way he proved himself right, as to this day that man still has no criminal record and never ever have we got any justice for his crimes.

At this time in our lives we had two horses with us in Ireland, we had brought them back from Spain, we had initially brought the boys ponies back but he made us sell them to a horrible home. When we went down to see the ponies they were not cleaned, they had cuts and abrasions on them, and were as nervous of people as you could get, these were not the ponies we had sold. On our way back from these stables, I and the boys were freaking at him. I have no idea how we got home alive, he was a total psychopath in the car and was going to punch my head through the driver side window. Of course when we eventually got home he did use his fists and then went out to the stables and sat drinking for the night He had no respect for me at all, especially if I had messed up or interfered with his plans.

Once again on a Sunday afternoon, I had dropped him to a pub at the back of Dublin Airport called The Boot Inn. He sometimes went there as it was far away from us. Anyway hours later I rang and rang and no answer to his mobile, this I knew was his stalling tactic and then he would say that his cell had no credit. So I put kids into my jeep at the time and drove to collect him. Well he freaked at me in the pub for walking in and saying come on we are going, but on the way home he started to hit me and punch me as I was driving. There was a phone unit in the car, he smashed it into my head and ripped my clothes, the kids were in the back he was like a wild animal. Somehow I managed to pull over and I got the kids out of the jeep and started to walk .I knew that we would never be able to walk home as it was so far away, and we were now walking on a motor way side path so dangerous., My shirt was ripped, I had mascara all down my face and nobody but nobody even stopped to ask if we were okay .It is not that it was normal in any way to see people walking on the motorway and especially not with a baby and three children. But they kept driving as did he .About five minutes into our walking he flew past us in the jeep, but went around the roundabout and went back to the pub for more drink. I called my dad and he very kindly drove to where we were and picked us up.

He was old school my dad and you just didn't hit or abuse your family he was so infuriated with Bas that he rang a cousin of his who was a Superintendent in the District that he lived in and told him what had happened. But again same old story unless he was caught in the act they could do nothing. Getting away with so much for so many years actually enabled him to escalate his abuse to the level that it eventually got to. The problem is that when you are caught in the abuse cycle it is very hard to get out of it. Yes we all say as soon as he hits you or as soon he keeps upsetting you, this is when you should walk away, but life is not always that easy.

Bas always had a really bad mouth on him and in particular when he was in a rage, he would say some of the most horrific and vile things that you could imagine. His favorite was that he would make sure that I would piss into a bag and be fed through a tube for the rest of my life. I mean this itself beggars belief, how can any man wish that on his wife the mother of his children, but people like Bas don't have a conscience. They only care about themselves and what they can control. At this stage in my life I had started to sleep with two steak knives under my pillow, one in each hand as I hugged the pillow at night. And then for back up I always had a bottle of bleach spray down the side of my mattress so that if I needed to I could spray that in his eyes. Thankfully I never used the knives or spray and he didn't know that they were there.

Yet when I think about it if I had taken the knives out he probably would have used them against me, as physically he was as strong as an ox, If somebody was to take him down then they would have to have a lot of others with them, as he was always so pumped up on adrenalin, anger, alcohol and probably some other stuff, but I that I don't know that for sure. The veins on his neck and arms would stand out as if he was flexing them for bodybuilding and that was without him tensing them. The amount of times that he tried to kill me in particular to strangle me, I have lost count of, as I should really be dead right now. But for some reason I have managed to survive, perhaps the reason for my survival was to tell my story, and to help other victims of abuse, to get the courage, to get the help and to get the hell away from their abuser.

Whether it is a man or woman who is the one causing all the pain in the home, nobody deserves to live a life of abuse. We get one shot at life, just one. When we die we die, we don't have the option to return and to relive our lives so that we can do things differently. If we want our life to be different then we ourselves must change it. And as hard as it will be in some cases to do this, we are the only ones who can.

Of course there are lots of agencies out there that could have helped us and our children. But like anybody who has an addiction to alcohol or drugs, in order to move on in their lives, in order to take back their own lives, they have to want it and really want it, at any cost .And its only then that you can start to take back the control that you once lost, and then in time you will get your life as you want it to be. It will not be as it was before the abuse, as you will have changed so much. But the strength that you find, to get you and your family out of that situation, is the strength that you will now draw on in order to have the life that you and your family want and more importantly deserve.

By this stage in our life, he was a full blown alcoholic, there is no two ways about it, although if I or the boys said anything to him about his drinking, well he would flip. Every day the first thing that he would do, would be to go to the fridge, then straight down to the loo and sit on the loo drinking his cans of cider .He had gone now from the spirits to the cider as he couldn't afford the luxury of the spirits, yet the cider was selling for something like five cans for Euro 6 about roughly USD 4, so it was a cheap way to get drink. I would find empty cans all over the place, behind the toilet, behind the sofa, under the bed, in the stables, in boot of the jeep. You could literally think of any place either in the house or the gardens and I guarantee you that I'd find drink there.

Things though by now had really escalated, there wasn't a day that went by that he didn't start some form of argument .Walking on egg shells was no longer, it was walking on cotton wool and even at that he would still fly off the handle. One of my sons Jake who was always my protector and the one who would stand up to him no matter what, had started now to sleep during the day and to staying up at night as he was so afraid as to what Bas would do to me when they were all asleep.

Jake wasn't getting on well in school and his principle was so horrible to him and would take any opportunity to make him feel like a piece of dirt, that he just didn't want to go into school, not that one anyway. As much as he wanted to learn and wanted to do well, with all of the constant hassle and abuse at home and all of the normal problems in school, it was just too hard for him to try and deal with it all. I told the school about the problems, but like in so many schools around the world, if a certain teacher or person working in the school takes a disliking to you ,there isn't much you can do .As you are going to be bullied and made out to be the villain whilst your there. Solely as they have the power and the control to do so, again this in my eyes is abuse.

Sadly though this is the reality, that is all too real for many children. They not only have to lead a life of abuse at home, but in school too. One day I had brought Jack and Mark to school, My eldest son Rory was at the house as was Bas. I was gone for less than a half an hour and when I came back I could see through the window, both Rory and Bas in Jakes bedroom and it was clear the two of them were in a rage. I ran into the house to hear Jake screaming at them. The two bastards and that's the only word that is even printable that I can call them, had him in a corner in his room they were punching and kicking the crap out of him, both of them against a 15 year old boy who was the son of one and the brother of the other. I grabbed both of them off Jake and freaked.

Rory stormed out and Bas stood at the door with that look in his eyes, even though he is not near me now, I can still see that evil look that is so evil, devious and dangerous that you know at that time that he is capable of murder. It still makes me shake totally uncontrollably inside and I hate it. Bas was so enraged that I stopped them beating Jake up, that he broke the handle off the bedroom door, it was an old style solid black curved steel handle and he threw it at me, he hit me right under my ribs. For a long time even though I was dressed when he threw it at me, I had the shape and bruising off this handle on my body.

Poor Jake was covered in bruises they kicked him, everywhere there wasn't a part of his body that they left untouched with their fists or toe capped boots. They meant business and the only way that they would get to him was if I wasn't there. They intended to do this, it wasn't something that just happened, it was planned and calculated, making what they did even worse.

When I calmed Jake down, he told me to look at the wardrobe door as it was all broken. When Bas went into Jakes room he grabbed him and threw him head first through the door, smashing the panels on the door of the wardrobe. Now the wardrobe was a solid Mexican pine one, so to break those panels into bits was done with some force. Jake hate for Bas at this stage was at an all- time high, he hated the man as much if not more than I did. Thinking that he might be sorry and that he might now realize that he needed help, I had hoped that his violence would stop, it didn't it never did.

He was short of money, we were struggling he wasn't working, there was no way on earth that I could leave the home. I knew that if I did, that I would come home to a dead body of one of at least one of the kids. And that something would for sure have happened to Jake, so I was restricted. There was no way that I would take the chance of harm coming to my son, nor give Bas and or Rory the opportunity to beat him up.

I was also now giving my dad full time care at this stage, as he had full blown cancer, it was at level 3 which is critical for any type of cancer. I was also caring for one of the boys, who had some medical problems. I wasn't sitting on my ass or drinking myself drunk everyday .My worst habit was sitting down and eating a full packet of biscuits ,with a mug of tea, that was the excitement in my life at the time. Anyway soon after the assault on Jake, there was just me and Bas in the house, Jack and Mark were at school, Rory was god knows where, and Jake was down the back at the stables with the two mares. All of a sudden Bas stormed in and told me that he wanted all of the horse tack that we had and that he was selling it all. I told him there was no way that he was doing that, as we would never be able to buy some of the equipment again.

My dad had bought tack that the kids had used in Spain, so that meant a lot to them. We didn't need the little bit of money that he would get for them that much, no he just wanted more money for drink. I hid stuff all around the house, he didn't know where most of it was but he caught me putting horse bandages and pads in the back of the hot press. The house we were living in at this time was a bungalow, so the press was in a corner in the hallway. He flipped he threw me against the wall, he wrapped his full arm around my neck and was choking me, this was it this time he was going to succeed.

How I prayed that Jake would come in and for some reason out of nowhere he appeared , he heard Bas shouting at me, so he knew that there was something wrong. He tried to pull him off me but the more he pulled the tighter he choked my neck. The two of us fighting against one man, with one arm around my neck and the other he was using to hit out at Jake, he was like a man possessed, there is no other way to describe him .I had very little strength at this stage, and couldn't get my arms up .I was trying to kick him but nothing, so the only thing that I could do was to bite him and god did I bite, I bit down on his arm so hard and so deep that he screamed.

He dropped me to the ground, and he pushed Jake out of the way, and the only thing that he could say was that I bit him. Right there and then I wished I could have killed him, as I knew that he had the strength, the will, and the determination to kill me, now it was just a matter of time before this happened. This particular rampage went on for days, he would go out get his drink come, back, and you would feel the darkness descend on the house, on us. We knew that we would have more of his crap again. He would always try and embarrass me especially in front of the boys, for some reason he enjoyed them and me been totally humiliated. His favorite thing to do in order to ensure maximum embarrassment would be to start slagging me about my body, about my genitals, but in graphic details. He would mimic me doing sexual acts and the most horrific to me, was him doing things with his hands and mouth that would make out that I was having oral sex. He would do this all the time, tell the boys that I was off having sex with other men and basically degrading me in the worst possible way. On one occasion he actually got a felt tip marker and wrote the words bitch, cunt, whore all over my naked body and showed my sons, I was never so degraded or humiliated in my life.

Jake and Mark decided to try and help me to protect Jack from as much of this as possible .He was still only a baby, well ten years old, but way too young for him to see any of this abuse, let alone the sexual abuse above. So the cloakroom which was in the hall-way was where they decided to hide him. At the back of it behind the coats, they put a small stool, with a torch and one of the house phones. When Bas would kick, off we would put him in there and although he could hear things, even with his hands on his ears he couldn't see them. It wasn't perfect but at the time it was all that we had to use. The scary thing was that if anybody and it didn't happen that often, but if family or friends would call down he would be as nice as pie. You would think that butter would melt in his mouth, when it was all an act, he should have won an Oscar for the acting that he performed.

One of his brothers knew that he was violent and abusive. He didn't know the full extent, but he knew enough. He did speak to him about it, but it made no difference. Actually in some ways it made it worse as he then thought that I was trying to take his brother away from him and to destroy their relationship, how wrong he was. I had wished so many times that his late mam was still alive. Irrespective of how tiny and petite as she was, or that she had lived a life of abuse herself, but she would have killed him for turning into his late dad. His dad was abusive to his mam, he was also an alcoholic but his abuse although it was horrific to Angel, it was nowhere near the level of his son. No Bas was in a league of his own, and unless he was stopped or we got away from him, then I would go from been a statistic to simply been another murder victim.

The headline news for all the newspapers in Ireland and this was not going to happen if I could help it. He had unknown to me been working with a company in the UK about emigrating to North America and they sent him a portfolio of information on this .He left it lying around, that's how I initially found out about it .But my dad was ill, there was no way that I was leaving him and going thousands of miles away, so it was just left by the side and not spoken about or thought about by me anyway. Bas finally got a job in Dublin Airport, Ireland re-fuelling the aircraft and he loved the job I now thought okay maybe this will settle him down, he was getting good money and loved the work and so he would have to stop drinking all day

I stupidly thought that he would change, well as they say a leopard doesn't change their spots and neither did Bas .Yes he did stop drinking during the day, well he was in work and they were randomly tested for drugs and alcohol, so he couldn't take the chance. However on his way home the first stop was the pub for at least a few hours, then drive home again with drink on him, with no regard for anybody else on the road. When he got home he would start his drinking again, so although in some ways he improved as he wasn't drinking 24/7, he was still drinking as much, just in a shorter period of time, there was still no escaping his abuse.

The only good thing other than him earning his wages, was that for whatever number of hours every day he was gone from the house, it meant that we had those hours in peace and that itself was the best feeling ever. It was as if the sun was shining inside the house for that period, but as soon as the gate opened, the darkness of fear and expectation fell on us once again, sadly we were never disappointed.

CHAPTER 9 – RORY BECOMES HIS DAD

They say that some abusers have literally learned their behavior and their actions from their own experiences in life. But that only relates to about 30% of those that have been abused as a child or grown up watching one parent abuse the other. As much as I do agree with this point in some ways, I don't in full. Some people I personally feel are actually born evil and devious from the day that they were conceived .As hideous and ridiculous in the eyes of some that may sound, I honestly believe that Rory was born the way he is today. Because no matter what I said or did, or what he saw happen in our home, the one thing that it should have done was to ensure that he never lived the way we did, and certainly never ever lift his hand or fist to another woman, especially not his wife or partner, or his own mam.

But after he joined his dad in kicking the crap out of his much younger brother at the time, I knew that he was his dad in waiting. If he was like him now it scared the hell out of me as to what he would be like in the future. Rory was my first born he is now 22 years old, and sadly I have no contact with him. I have no phone number, or address for him all that I know is that he lives I think somewhere in NYC. He is sadly not the person that I raised and neither I nor the boys have any contact with him. He is happy with that apparently I should according to him keep my mouth shut a bit more. But that's what I was forced to live like with my abuser for over 20 years, and that only enabled him to escalate to the level that he did.

So I am not going to stay quiet ever again, and will speak out about abuse until I have no voice left to do so. Rory was the image of me, the big eyes, the round face he was my twin .That used to bug Bas, as everybody would say it but that's life, as we have no control over who our kids will look like when their born that is not ours to decide. He was always a liar and a player from his early teenager years. I would always say that he should be on the Jerry Springer Show as he could tell a tale and make you believe it was true.

When he was 12 years old I brought him to Temple Street Children's Hospital in Dublin to see a specialist there .I had done a course in the hospital a few months prior to that on ADHD ,and general behavior problems in kids. From what I could see he suffered from Oppositional Deficit Disorder, which basically meant that if I said it was black he would say it was white. He always had to have the last say, always had to be assumed that he was the one in the right even if it was clear he was totally in the wrong.

I had to leave him with the specialist for about an hour as he was doing a test with him ,it was basically asking questions and seeing how he reacted to certain things. Well when I came back in to the room. Rory was smiling and the specialist was not happy at all. He began to freak at me, tearing strips off me for bringing my son in there as there was nothing wrong with him at all. He was perfect as far as he was concerned, I was gob-smacked in total shock, I didn't wish my son to have any problem but I sure as hell knew that he did have one. Now I looked the fool.

So I got Rory and we walked outside the clinic, just as we were walking up to the car he started to laugh, I will never ever forget it and he turned to me and said ha I fooled him now didn't I. To be honest I wasn't exactly sure as to what he meant, but he told me that he knew what answers the doctor wanted so gave them to him, he wasn't going to let me win. That day although now over ten years ago will stick with me forever and that day is one that terrified me, as it was then that I realized that my eldest son was his dad in more ways than one.

He was very close to my parents in particular mam, even though when he was a young baby she had very little to do with him. He was invisible to her sadly until he was about two years old. As I had got pregnant out of wedlock, but now they were very close. If he wanted something and I wouldn't get it for him then the next time he was up at his nanas and granddads he would ask and he would receive. Mam and I had many falling outs over this, she could see no wrong in giving him what he wanted, but what she didn't see was the side of him that for now he was controlling whilst in front of other people. But it was a side that when it shone through even my mam would have been shocked. I thank god that she died before she could see how he turned out sadly my dad was duped by him, but saw him for who he was eventually and that really broke his heart.

Rory was an amazing show jumper, when we were in Spain. He was jumping heights that those who had trained for years were only starting to attempt. He had the best of horses, all the gear that he required and the best instructors. He was we were told Olympic material maybe just maybe I had hoped this would put him on the right path. Unfortunately all it did was to make him money hungry and to think that unless you have money you are a nobody to him and that to me is very sad indeed.

He was in a huge competition that is held in the south of Spain every year in a town called Montemedio. He was there with his new trainer and his horse. There was an Irish show jumper there who was very well known, all around the world and who was very impressed by Rory. So much so that he offered to take him back to Ireland with him and to train him up to be a top class rider. In return Rory would work for him. At 15 this was a once in a lifetime opportunity, as much as I didn't want him to be in Ireland and us in Spain. If I had have said no then he would resent me for life, and if I said yes and it didn't work out the way he wanted, then I would be in the bad books, either way.

So we discussed it and agreed that he could go in a few weeks when he had finished his school year. When Rory went back to Ireland Bas went with him, god it was great just me and the three boys, no hassle, no fighting, no fear it was too good to last though. A few months later we ended up back in Ireland too. Rory would travel all over Europe with this trainer yes the hours were long and the work hard, but to experience all that he was learning that was invaluable. I could collect him from work at 2am and have to have him back there for 6 am, but as tiring as it was he was getting his dream or so I thought.

Sometime after he started his job we moved back to Bas old

home town, it was by no means my choice rather the sensible one as closer to dads house and closer to the town where Rory worked, also to the kids schools. So for now it was the viable option. We were only there a short period of time when Rory started going out with a girl from the town. Now our door was always open even with the abuse from Bas. We knew if people always coming and going, then we would have that more time without his temper. But for some reason she never ever was allowed to meet us, never allowed to come into the house. We had many arguments with him over this, as she would pull into the driveway in the car that her parents had bought her and just beep the horn, then he would simply walk out and was gone. After a long time it started to annoy us all, it was as if we weren't good enough for her. She apparently came from a wealthy family, but so what money is here today gone tomorrow we all know that, but family we are meant to be forever. One night she did come into the house and I met her it was a brief hello, then into his room to watch TV. After about an hour they just went out and that was the one and only time that she was in our house.

Rory was still working at the stables and the hours were really long. His girlfriend was not happy that he was working so many hours .But I heard him on the phone to her one day talking about his college course, and how he was exhausted been in college and then working and riding. I thought that either id lost my mind or it was somebody else talking, as he wasn't in college he was at the stables and that was it. Now it was clear he was lying to impress her, I told him that if she truly loved him, that she would love him whether he was in college or not, and that if she didn't well then he was better off without her ,he wasn't impressed.

One day Bas got a call from Rory's boss at the stables asking him to meet him for a chat. Apparently he had caught Rory lying on a number of occasions and he just couldn't seem to get through to him. Even when he proved that he had lied, Rory didn't want to know. His boss was so infuriated that Rory had brought his girlfriend down the night before, and showed her the inside of the horse truck that he used to live in when away. They were apparently caught by somebody doing something sexual in the truck, so Rory was on a serious warning, and I had hoped that now he would just concentrate on his work and not about his love life.

It so happened that a few weeks later Bas had to go down to Spain to sort out the villa there, as it was up for sale and some squatters had got into it, so he was going to get rid of them and fix the garden. He brought Jake and Mark with him as they would be a great help and they loved going down there and spending time with our Spanish friends, who were more like family then friends. I knew that they would be safe there the problem was although I thought I was safe, I was to be proven so wrong, my son had become his dad.

On the Friday night Rory went out with his girlfriend, there was only myself and Jack in the house. We did the usual and watched a movie then went to bed. However Rory was due into work at 5am, so as he was only 16 years old at this stage, I told him to be in before midnight .With some jobs you can get away with having little or no sleep, but when you are dealing with and caring for horses, you need your brain to be in full working order and you cannot make a mistake .If you do then you will either end up hurt, or somebody else will, perhaps even worse the poor horse will get ill, so it was critical that he got his sleep and acted responsible.

I got a text back from him telling me to Fuck Off and that he would be in when he was in. Now I flipped I told him to get in but no use, the texts kept coming .Then the girlfriend text me telling me that I was trying to break them up, all id wanted was for him to get to bed at a decent hour, so that he could go to work and do his job and for some reason this was wrong to expect of him. When he did come home it was about 1.30am, and Jack was fast asleep .Rory's bedroom and bathroom was downstairs so there was no need for him to come up the stairs, unless he wanted something and he wanted me. He wanted to teach me a lesson my own son. I got out of my bed when I heard him coming up the stairs, well bounding up them and met him at my bedroom door his eyes were scary.

I knew he had taken something, his pupils were huge and he was in a rage. He pushed me back and grabbed me around the neck, he went onto throw me around the bedroom onto my bed. I knocked the lamp down and everything beside it here, I was been strangled again, yet this time by the child that I had carried and given birth to. I was in tears and screaming at him, but he didn't hear me he was intent on stopping me have any say in his life. I managed to get my arms up, even though he had me in a choke hold and I scrapped the face off him. It stopped him, he got up and just pushed me back onto the bed ,I knew that if Bas had of been there that this wouldn't have happened ,as although he physically abused me he thought that was his right and he wasn't going to let somebody else especially not his own son take his fun away.

But what happened next to this day still devastates me .But like everything in life that we endure somehow we learn to deal with it. He walked back into my room and said watch this, I'm going to ring grand-dad. Now my dad was on Chemo he was really ill and was exhausted, in bed asleep, it was after all nearly 3am at this stage. No Rory didn't care he wanted to hurt me and he wasn't going to stop until he did. He rang my dad and as soon as the phone was answered he started to cry, but what dad couldn't see was the smile on his face. He told my dad that id assaulted him that everything he had done to me apparently, I had done to him, I was in shock, not only had my son violently assaulted me, now he was lying through his teeth to my terminally ill dad, knowing that it would destroy me and cause a lot of friction between us.

When he hung up the phone, he simply turned to me laughed and said now that shut you up didn't it. I was literally stuck for words it was like a bad dream, I think I was in a daze as it was all so unreal. However I was woken from this daze, when the phone rang and it was my dad screaming and shouting at me over Rory. Knowing how ill my dad was and how close we were this broke my heart. I ended up hanging up on him, sadly our relationship for a long time after that was not the same.

The next day was a Saturday and he hadn't gone into work he had called in sick or something .Anyway he took the stairs down for the attic and started to walk around up there throwing things about. I told him to be careful as it wasn't a floored attic and if you walk on the wrong spot your through the ceiling. He just hurled abuse at me. He got the bags that he was looking for, put a lot of his stuff into it and stormed out the front door, I watched him go up the road and for my brother to meet him and to put him into his car and they drove away to dads house.

Family war broke out, I text my brother as I was so infuriated at his actions, he didn't even have the decency to call or to text me to ask what the problem was. No Rory had them all convinced that I had done to him, what he had in actual fact done to me. I told Pat what had happened and that he was been played, that Rory simply wanted to be up at dads for more freedom and so that he could be on his insurance and to drive the car. Within days that is exactly what he got. Pat text me back that I had lost my son the day that I had started to abuse him and that I would not be allowed to abuse my children anymore. Now I had not been the abuser Bas was and all the kids knew that and so did Pat, my parents had told him, but no he was been played and lying was to be one of Rory's best works of art and still is .Not only did he get a new part-time job in Bewleys Hotel at Dublin Airport, he was now apparently going back to school, he was going to go to the Institute of Education .A top class very expensive private school, I told my dad that he was wasting his money that he would only go for a while and that he wouldn't stick it out. He had done this twice before with us in private schools, so I knew it would only be a matter of time and it was.

Dad would drop and collect him at all hours of the day and night from his job and eventually put him on the car insurance so that he now had full use of his car. With no parents to tell him what to do, and a Granddad with a heart of gold that was been fooled by him and everybody else been played all for his own gain. His lies and abuse escalated. He stayed at the school for about six months, I think then he was working more and more until finally he just wasn't bothered going to school and his grand-dad lost the money he had invested in him.

I couldn't say I told you so, but he knew that I had been right all along. Rory continued to stay at dads it was company for him, as well so in that sense I didn't mind. Thankfully dad and I were now on talking terms again, but Rory by now had his girlfriend calling up to dads and doing the same thing beeping from outside. Dad felt so caught in the middle and as if his life wasn't hard enough dealing with the cancer, that was progressing around his body at extremely fast levels, at 76 years old he didn't need any more hassle or upset Things were so bad between Rory and us all in his family, that he would drive past us in the town where we lived, with or without the girlfriend and ignore us, even his little brothers.

It made me sick, it still does .There were many times when I went to the police over their behavior and they also apparently went about me, as I was harassing the girlfriend, according to Rory the liar. As
the actual truth about what happened was a lot different to his and her lies and bullshit. She worked in the local shop where we lived and I told her one of the days that I didn't care what she and Rory did, but to stay away from my terminally ill dad's house, as he was terminally ill and that I wouldn't stand for him been upset. Her doing what she had done at our house with the car beeping from outside not even ringing the door bell, this really distressed my dad which was totally understandable. She rang

the police and filed a complaint, nothing was done as I had done no wrong. Eventually they broke up and Rory got a full time job as a chef out in the infamous Luttrellstown Castle Hotel and Golf Course. It is famous for been the venue to host the marriage of Posh & Beck's, he had now still no car and was using dads. I still have no idea as to how he got a job as a chef ,as he had gone in as a kitchen porter when he was in Bewley's.

Apparently however a chef there had taken him under his wing and somehow created a miracle and made him into a chef. He worked there for many years and in time found his own car, he then heard that they were reportedly closing down so he left. However that didn't happen and he regretted leaving there for many years. He then got a job in another part of Dublin and ended up meeting another girl. She then also ended up getting tangled in his web of deceit, this web, which I didn't think could ever get worse than it was. Eventually he went to a level that in some ways was as bad if not worse than Bas.

At this stage he had moved home as it was too stressful for my dad then sadly just a few months after Rory moved home, my lovely dad died, in my arms in my bed in my home. He was where he wanted to be. I don't even think I saw one tear from Rory over the man who had given him all that he had and more. Yet now all he could do was to tell all his friends and his girlfriend that his grand-ads house was actually his and that he was loaded with money.

To me it is sad when the only thing that motivates you in life to do anything is money, as far as I am concerned, yes it is great to have some and not to have worries, but it will never ever buy happiness all that it will buy is trouble. Things between Rory and his girlfriend moved fast actually way too fast, I initially met her and she seemed nice enough, at least we actually met this one and from my first impression she was just a normal girl, no airs, or graces, about her. But to me they didn't fit ,as he was the opposite to her then again they say opposites do attract .Within a few weeks she was staying over the night with him, then it was more than one night and in time it turned into a permanent fixture. Apparently things at home had been hard for her, she was the only girl and there were different types of addictions in the family. She was tired of all the rows, so with them both working in the same place, it was easier for her to stay with him and come and go to work together. After a few months they ended up renting an apartment in Dublin City near Heuston Station that was a big mistake. I told them that from the start, but all they could see was the flash apartment and no rules and freedom, I guess we have all been there at some stage.

I knew by then that they were both smoking weed. I never let any type of smoking in my house, and certainly not what I consider a drug it just wasn't allowed .I was made out to be the fool but I knew what the smell was and them always having money, I even found their little stash one day, when I was getting something from his car. Jake hated her from the start, he can read any person like a book within minutes of meeting them, and he is very seldom wrong. If he says their trouble generally he is right and he didn't like Mary in anyway at all, the feeling was by then mutual.

So they moved out into their apartment and for a few weeks all was fine, then the fights started, mostly about his working long hours. By now he was working in Dublin City, and she was still in her home town, So they were on different shifts, and at times they wouldn't see each other for a day or so. Rory would be not only drinking after work, but before it and during it in his coffee mugs. Sadly he is now at 22 an alcoholic like his dad. He says he isn't , but when the first thing you do in the morning is grab your giant travel mug and fill it with Patron, which is a tequila you have a problem whether you want to accept it or not.

Apparently he was seen by some friends of Mary in a bar with another girl and they were both all over each other, so of course she flipped. He denied it and this went on for a number of weeks One night in that December, he rang me in a hysterical state about 4am in the morning. He said that she was up in the apartment and wouldn't let him in, but that she had her ex- boyfriend there and lots of other friends and they wanted to beat the crap out of him over this apparent other girl.

I told him to ring the police and to stay put not to attempt to go into the apartment alone. Eventually the police arrived and the entire apartment had been thrashed, it was like a bomb site. There was make-up and creams that were all squeezed on to the carpets, the kitchen was the dirtiest smelliest kitchen, I have ever seen it was disgusting. All his clothes and belongings thrown around, all hers on ground too. His cookery books ripped it was pure vandalism and destruction, no other way to describe it. The police were sending a forensics team the next morning, so I said I'd meet them there, as Rory wasn't well enough to deal with it, he was having panic attacks.

When the forensics guys went I started to clean up the place with Mark, who had come with me to help. It took over eight hours to clean a one bed apartment. However when we were cleaning, we found a lot of items that I am sure we were not meant to, and I realized that one or perhaps both were dealing weed from the apartment. We found a scales, lots of small bags with weed sign on them a list with names and more importantly an I phone with text messages asking for certain amounts of weed, or texts saying where to meet. It was clear even to me who didn't know that much about drugs ,that this was not right .I dumped all the paraphernalia that I found and threw them in the rubbish bags, I didn't care if they didn't like it, I wasn't going to tolerate drugs and that was that.

I didn't want to keep the phone, so I gave it to somebody that I knew in the Drug Task Force and who I knew would do something with it. When I showed him the texts he agreed that they were indeed deals that had been set up, and orders been made. Rory stayed on in the apartment alone for a while, I had packed her stuff and with police present gave it all out to her and her brothers and mam. That I had hoped was the last of it, but this is my family nothing is ever that simple. By now Rory was home with us, he couldn't afford the apartment alone and it was the only viable solution, plus I could keep an eye on him.

One day she text me to tell me that she was sorry, that she was devastated, that they had broken up, she didn't know what to do and that she was pregnant .I nearly died as this was a dread that I had within me and now it had happened .She told me that she was getting lots of hassle off her family and didn't know what she should do. She said that she still loved Rory and didn't understand as to why he could just dump her, he must never have loved her, I wasn't surprised as he had become his dad, the violence, the drinking, the lies and the drugs now the pregnancy it was a real Deja- vu. My heart told me to ring her, my head said stay away but I knew what it was like to be young and pregnant and to be alone. As much as I didn't like her I felt for her, so I made that call .I spoke to her for hours and this went on for a long period of time. However I was also concerned that the child she was pregnant with was not Rory's, as I had also seen texts in the I phone, that id taken that made me question who the dad was.

I was extremely concerned over the fact that the baby would be born in agony going through cold turkey if she and Rory as I had realized that they were both smoking weed and or doing other drugs, as I really did not know what they were both into fully. Her relationship with my son was hot and cold, and after a lot of talking to them, they got back together. She moved for a short while back into our house. Then one Saturday morning Rory just turned around without notice and said that they were looking at a house to rent in the town and would be moving out as soon as possible,

I was furious at the fact that they just dumped this on me and also the fact that I didn't know how they would be able to manage rent, utilities and a baby it just didn't make sense. They moved out within the week and I tried to help them as much as possible. He was off working and she was stuck in the house pregnant ,with no friends, no family, and no car, so I really felt for her .I just wanted to try to help as much as they would let me ,I got her registered with my doctor and helped her clean the house. I was going to the supermarket one day and rang her phone to see if she wanted to get a break from the house and just come with me or if she wanted me to get her some groceries, if she wasn't up to it.

She didn't answer, well her phone answered, but she must not have realized as I heard her argue with Rory over me. She told him that she didn't move to this area for another nagging mother,and that I was only a cunt and was driving her mad. To say that my temper was boiling is an understatement, I was fuming, id taken her back into the family after all that had happened, and had only tried to help her and this was what she thought of me, I rang Rory he in all honesty didn't get to say one word as I was screaming at him so much, but I was shaking with temper ,how dare she. At that moment I knew I had made a huge mistake by helping them get back together but now I was stuck with it .But if I couldn't be around my son, as he was with Mary ,then I was going to make sure that the baby was okay. No baby asks to be born and no baby should have to endure any type of pain because of the actions of their parents. I text Mary and Rory and I told them that their baby did not ask to be made and that if the baby was conceived whilst they were smoking their weed or any other drugs, then it would be born in agony.

It would be born in cold turkey or worse handicapped and if it was going to suffer because of their actions, then it would be better off not been born. I was later told that this meant I wished the baby dead .I didn't I love babies, but a little baby to be born suffering one of the worst conditions that is possible to me is unthinkable .It would also suffer possibly problems all its life over their actions. I rang the maternity hospital and told them my concerns. I knew that Rory and Mary would freak, but at this stage I didn't care what they thought of me, as all they thought about was them-selves.

Within five months of meeting they were living together, doing their dealing of weed and god knows what else and now pregnant it just was too much too fast. After that, they stopped all contact, not even my own son spoke to anybody in the house for months, his own family he just dumped. Actually we found out that the baby was born through friends on Facebook, but that was done to cause as much upset and distress as possible. Other than a photo by phone, we have not seen this child. I have no idea if it is my son's baby and if it is then it is my grandchild, but as he dumped her within weeks of the birth unsurprisingly, this is something that we still some years later do not know.

The baby as far as I can see is not his, as there are family traits that all the family even extended have and he looks the image of her ex boyfriend. I don't know and probably never will know as Rory is not around in Ireland and he doesn't like his dad pay child support either .He did sign the birth cert, but told me later that he didn't think the baby was his. I have no answers to my questions as much as I would love to have the child in my life if he is my grandchild. I don't want his mams family anywhere near mine, I don't want to be involved or connected with them so what do I do. For now I will stay away as the little boy seems to be growing up into a little man and if my son is his dad, well to be honest he is better off without him in his life, as if he was there as a dad all the child would learn is how to lie, cheat, drink and abuse others. So in some ways it is the right thing for this baby to be kept away from our family. I don't regret what I said to his girl-friend, as the only person I was concerned with was the baby and as he at the time couldn't stand up for himself, so I was dam well going to do it for him. Right or wrong my intentions were solely for the baby to be born safe and well. From what I have seen of his photos he seems to be thriving.

Mary lives with another man as far as I am aware, and in my opinion he is looked on by the child as daddy. But anybody can make a child it takes a man to rear one, so if it is my sons baby and he is the one supporting him and rearing him then in my eyes he is the daddy. Rory has no right to claim that title solely cause his sperm may have made the child. He abandoned this baby if it is indeed his and that is in my opinion disgusting.

He was due in court in the January for non-payment of child support actually the date was my birthday, so I will never forget it. The night before he was meant to stay at my house and get himself up and ready early. Yet late that night when the rest of us had gone to bed he had text me to say that the was staying in his own house and would be down early next morning, I knew he was lying but he was an adult it was his life, so I just went back asleep. The next morning he text and called me that he was on the way to my house. About 20 minutes later, I got a call from his phone but from a stranger, he told me that Rory had been in a car crash, I could hear him in the background, crying and saying I want my mam, I jumped into the car and flew to the scene, how I managed to get there in one piece or without been stopped for speeding, I will never know.

When I arrived at the scene, I saw a massive tail back, I drove the wrong side of the road in order to get to my son. All that I saw was a car that was disintegrated and a blanket over the driver my son .I screamed and ran to him the fire brigade pulled me back, but all I could see was that my son was dead .Thankfully he wasn't but they had to cover him up, until they could cut the roof off the car as they couldn't get him out any other way. After what seemed like an eternity he was put into the ambulance, he was screaming with pain in his stomach, he had not one mark or cut on his body that I could see. The scary thing was that one of the ambulance men looking after Rory knew me. I didn't recognize him at first, but he was an ex-boyfriend of Bas niece. I hadn't seen him in years, but it was weird that I saw him for the first time when he is trying to save my sons life and how he did. When we got to Beaumont Hospital we were rushed into the Critical Care area, this gave me goose bumps as it was in the same bed, same cubicle, that Jake had been in two years prior to that when he was on life support, in a coma. I couldn't believe that here I was again.

The doctors gave him lots of meds for the pain but nothing was hitting it .They had him on a spinal board and in a collar until they did x-rays .We went to x-ray department and as I sat outside I heard him screaming in pain. As a mam I just wanted to run into him, I had forgotten about all the hassle and crap that had gone on over the years this was my son. Eventually after what seemed like hours but was probably only 40 minutes they brought him back to the critical area. The doctor told us that his back and neck were fine and that he would be taken off the board and collar now. But there was something not right, he was screaming in agony, now he is a wimp at the best of times and no use for pain, but he was genuinely in agony and nobody seemed to care.

A junior doctor came in to check him and I told him that I wasn't happy that with all the medication in my son, that he should be out cold or definitely not in pain. He agreed and said that he would take a look at the x-rays himself, now this was a junior doctor in training The doctor who had looked at the original x-ray was qualified, then within minutes there was a fuss and a senior doctor came in and told Rory not to move a muscle. That he had to stay still from the neck down as he had broken his back and that he had shattered part of the bones.

Thankfully they went the opposite side to the spinal cord as if not he would have been paralyzed for life .They were considering moving him to the Mater Hospital as it had a specialist spinal unit there, but the move was too dangerous that's how unstable his spine was. Yet they had sat him up, taken him off the board and removed his neck collar in the critical care area. I was infuriated, how did we know that they hadn't now paralyzed him, or caused more damage .I went over to the nurse station and nobody was available .So I went to the reception in the main part of the hospital and demanded to speak to somebody. I was told to go back to A & E and that I would be contacted there .A short while later a very heavily nurse came out to me. I told her what had happened and how enraged that I was, yet her words stunned me. I was told that it was not coronation street (A soap on TV) and to stop been a drama queen.

I couldn't believe my ears, not only had they possibly paralyzed my son, now I was been told I was fussing over nothing. This type of care continued in the hospital. Even after he had spinal fusion surgery they messed up .He suffers from severe Anaphylactic Shock and therefor had to have non egg based anesthetic this was marked on his file in big print. The surgical team came up they spoke to us and verified all of the above would be done, then when he goes down to surgery not only is he told by the nurse there that he has no allergies, she also said that he would be having surgery on an artery in his leg.

They had the wrong file for him, after all that had happened in A & E here they were again making inexcusable mistakes, if he had of been zonked on the medication their negligence ,would have killed him. As he would not have been able to speak to them and tell them they had the wrong file. He was sent home about a week later with rods and pins holding his back in place ,they never so much as gave me a wheelchair for him or a bed pan it was all left to me and Jake to do. Suddenly I was now a providing full time care for two members of my family, and other than my own doctors I'd have been totally lost.

We had no help, I lived about a 30 minute drive from Beaumont Hospital and he was both unable to sit and terrified to get into a car. They should have organized home physiotherapy at the very minimum, but instead insisted that he go to the hospital for same. It was neither possible nor viable. So as Rory was now back in our home, we did everything for him. From helping him move in the bed, to helping him go to the toilet, other than move his head and arms he was totally immobile and literally just dumped for us to deal with.

The wound wasn't as big as I would have expected, however it was right on his spine. Apparently he had extensive internal bruising so it was excruciating for him. The wound was infected but not surprisingly as he hadn't been put on any antibiotics after surgery just painkillers. That smell was so horrific, it was like pure sewage and the puss that was oozing out was a green color.

We had stupidly assumed that a district nurse would be sent in to our home to clean and dress the wound daily, but again no, it was my job to play nurse. After about a week of this horrific puss, I managed to get him to our doctors .It was a simple 15 min drive, yet took me over an hour, as I literally had to crawl. Any car he saw he would shake uncontrollably, it was very hard to see. My doctor gave him antibiotics and gave me some dressings, in time the wound healed and despite the expectations of all that it would be at least 18 months before he was up and walking again, we managed to do it in a lot less and that was without the hospital help.

His ex-Mary knew about the accident. I had text her more out of decency, than anything else as it was such a serious accident that I felt she should know. More fool me, I simply got a text with a ha- ha in it and telling me that she hoped that I had to wipe his butt for life, and that it couldn't have happened to a nicer person. As according to her, I had wished her baby dead .I didn't wish the baby dead, I had said that if the baby was been born depended on drugs that she took, then it would have been kinder for the baby not to have been born just to suffer.

At this stage I thought that perhaps after all that he had gone through, and all that we had done for him in the family that perhaps he would have seen the error of his ways, and changed back to the person id hope he would become. Little did I know that he was still playing his games, and he was still lying to me and to us all. I will never know if what he told us that he remembered about the accident was right or wrong, as I don't believe a word out of his mouth, but if that accident and his injuries did not wake him up and knock sense into him, than there was nothing that would.

He was particularly quiet this one Wednesday and it didn't make any sense. His phone was ringing non-stop and he was texting or talking on it to who I didn't know. He then called me into his room where he was still in a wheelchair, unable to walk, unable to bend and unable to sit .But he proceeded to tell me that at 8am the next morning he was on a flight to New York to meet his old boss, who was a legendary scam artist yet famous chef from Ireland. This chef had now sought refuge in the USA, after all he had too many people here in Ireland where after him, including the Revenue Commissioners and he was dragging my son into his web of deceit and scams.

I totally flipped out at this but there was no telling him, yet he was back home within 7 days. When he got there it had been all lies and he was left with his bags and crutches to hobble around New York, with no money looking for a hostel to stay in, he for now anyway coped on and was back in Ireland. Within days he just upped and got a plane home didn't even tell the chef, after all why should he. So he came back to mammy and his brothers, and back to his been taken care of and having no worries but I could see his old ways sneaking in they were slowly been done, but obvious enough. He was so mean with his money, he still is to this day, he doesn't care what anybody spends on him or on his needs, once he doesn't have to spend it he is happy with that.

His life was then taken control off, by the chef months later and what he has become now and who he has become is somebody who I don't ever want in my life again. As cold and hard as that sounds, my son is totally brainwashed by this man, not only has he the learned behavior from his dad which is horrific enough, he now also has the learned behavior and all the scams from this chef and his partner in crime in New York another Irish Man.

So really my son is worse, than the man who I called my husband. Any chance we had of rescuing him from the clutches of been an abuser in life has been taken from us .He is now in the hands of a man that is evil and so sly that he would hang anybody out to dry once his ass is covered .

CHAPTER 10 – JAKE MY MIRACLE

Jake was always the hardest of all my children, not that he was giving trouble, but even as a baby in the womb he would have what my Doctor called attacks similar to asthma and the funny thing was even though I never smoked he was born chronic Asthmatic .I had an amazing Gynaecologist a Dr Miriam Brennan, the first time that I heard her voice on the phone I nearly died, she sounded so scary and would answer her phone the same way every time with one word that was so exaggerated, she would say Yesssssssss. But she was the nicest kindest and most fantastic of doctors that I had ever had and I was totally confident in her care.

I was going to have him in Holles Street Hospital one of the main maternity hospitals in Ireland, She was well known and very well respected there, all the nurses were terrified of her and would look at me funny if I answered her back or said something smart ,but she always laughed and she was amazing .Of course I was in and out of the hospital through-out the pregnancy and then went over by about a week, I had seen her on the Tuesday in her rooms and she told me that she had a big golf tournament the next day and that I was not to go into labor on the Wednesday, as she didn't want to miss the golf.

All of a sudden I got this pit in my stomach and I knew that I would go into labor on the day she made me promise not to. Next day low and behold labor I went into. She was given the call by the staff whilst she was on the course, I was terrified of her coming in, but there was nothing that I could have done, the little demon had made sure to make his mark in the womb, now he was doing it on delivery. I knew then that I was guaranteed that in life he would do the same and he has proven me right every time. When Dr. Brennan walked into the labor ward, I didn't know whether to laugh or cry, but she laughed so that broke the ice and within about 40 minute's trouble was born. He was a big baby 8lb 9oz and was as noisy then as he is today.

He had eyelashes that you would die for and those big balluba lips as I call them, he was going to be a looker hence all the trouble with him prior to been born, he was giving us fair warning. He was in and out of hospital for the first two years of his life. I ended up leaving work to mind him as it was just so unfair to him for me to be constantly running around and it was unfair to my bosses who had been extremely good to me all along. No I had to stop work in travel and start real work as mammy. I have no idea as to the amount of times that I was in and out of Temple Street, his Pediatrician Dr. John Murphy was great he was very similar in his mannerism to Dr. Brennan, but an excellent doctor and I trusted him totally, He diagnosed Jake with persistent bronchiolitis and he was on inhalers and medication every few hours, when he wasn't an in-patient it was hard as with Rory at home I was trying to juggle them both, but we got there you always seem to in the end. He was a little demon, Dennis the menace had nothing on him there wasn't a curtain that he wouldn't swing out of or a wall high enough to stop him jumping off, and the energy of a Duracell battery.

I was asked on one occasion in the hospital day ward to take him out of the ward as he was upsetting all the other babies. He was jumping around so much in the cot, the funny thing was this was after his pre-med for surgery to remove a cyst on his eyelid, I had told the staff that the dosage of 5ml that they gave him wouldn't work as he was on over 20 ml of that medicine at night just to try and to get him to sleep. They were wasting their time, but they didn't listen and he didn't calm down it was so embarrassing having been asked to remove my baby from a ward, he was only 18 months old and could hardly walk and talk yet was disrupting an entire ward, what the hell was he going to be like in the future.

When he went to theatre, I went in and as they usually do they tell the child count to 20 then you will be asleep, than they get the parent to say bye-bye. Well I did that and as I am walking out the door he jumps up on the bed and shouts mammy, well I don't know who had more of a shock me, the nurse, the anesthetist or the doctor after that they listened to me re how hyper he was. The years just flew by and we were in and out of the hospital, so many times that they knew him by name .He would do things he saw on TV like a jackass stunt, once sliding down steps in a barrel he very nearly killed himself, but he thought it was great fun.

However when he was old enough to realize that what went on in our house with his dad was not normal, that is when he really started to find his voice and find his inner strength .I don't even think he knew that it was there, it was this strength that to me was the one thing that pulled him out of a coma when he was just 15 years old.

He had started as most teenagers do at some stage to mess about with drink, most of the kids and teenagers in the town we lived in would go to the beach or to the woods and drink, mainly at the weekends or on Bank Holidays. I didn't want him drinking at all and I was so scared that he would like Rory turn in to his dad. Having one son become his dad was bad enough, having two that was just unthinkable. We still didn't' know all that Bas had been involved with over the years and I am sure that we never will be. Some people from outside the town that Bas knew from when he was apparently dealing some years ago, suddenly appeared in to our lives and decided that he owed them money. They made a point of this been said directly to Jake, I wasn't there when this was actually said to him, and it was a long time before I found out what was really going on.

He was getting very moody and very angry at everything and everybody and he hated Bas so much. I was terrified if they got into an argument as he was now very strong and muscular and his adrenalin rush to stop Bas was as bad as Bas adrenalin rush to kill me. School was just a nightmare he was told by the principal on one occasion that he would never be anything in life and that he would end up in jail, Now what she didn't know that he taped her on his mobile, stating this on one occasion. After all he was just a kid and when she denied saying this to my son in a subsequent meeting, we let the persons that mattered outside of the school here her tape. They then knew that she was a liar and they knew then that in that particular school, my son would have no chance with this attitude towards him.

We moved him at 15 to a VEC Youth Reach School in a nearby town. The reference that he got from that school from the teachers and the principal showed that the problem was not my son it was the woman who wanted to be seen as doing good for the old school when in fact all that she was doing was running a dictatorship. Everybody was afraid to stand up to her including the teachers as they said to me, they needed their jobs and they shouldn't have to be in fear of losing them, just for standing up for a child that was been victimized by the school and in particular the principal.

Now her hatred and that is what it was for my son and for me for standing up for him was so bad that she tried to put a claim against him through one of the teachers for sexual harassment. If my son so much as touched anybody, for in an inappropriate sexual manner, I would personally bring him to the police. But what happened shows her level of desperation. He was in detention and there was a song that was been played in the school hall which was beside the detention room. This was a song that contained a lot of sexual innuendos, but it was been played over the school speakers so somebody okayed it. Anyway he started to sing the song, he shouldn't have but he sang the song and the teacher wrote that down as sexual harassment. I flipped when I heard this, I went to the Dept of Education and the police everywhere, but as usual in Ireland either the laws aren't actually broken, or the laws just aren't there. So again he was a victim, just like we had been all our lives

I moved him to his new school and it proved that the problem wasn't my son it was the management of the previous school. There were a lot of older people in the Youth Reach, after all it is for older kids and they initially took him under their wing. But that is how the people who Bas owed money to found out where he was. They put two and two together. I would drop him to school and collect him every day and an odd day he would get the bus home for some independence, but in general he was collected by me.

Then he started staying late, always getting delayed and he himself changed .It was like he had the weight of the world on his shoulders. In our home town he was hanging around with a lad that is a total piece of scum, but they had been friends since kindergarten. At the time he couldn't see what I did, he was bad news and I knew that as long as my son was around him he would be in danger. At the same time now there seemed to be trouble at school. One day on my way to collect him, I went into the ATM in the shop beside were we lived and went to take out money. I knew I had money on my card, but my card wasn't in my bag, I had put it there the night before. I rang the bank and they told me that the card had been used that morning in the same town as the school and that a 100 Euro had been withdrawn. I cancelled the card there and then.

I was literally foaming at the mouth with anger, my son, the one who was so close to me had stolen from me, that was not him .He would ask me if he needed money, I knew there was more to it. When I got to the school it was closed, nobody was about so I walked the streets. I walked the town the housing estates and the park .Eventually some kids told me that they knew where he was or at least who he was with, and in the end after hours of searching I found him in a different town. He had managed to get the bus to where he thought was safe, but they had followed him and I had just missed these thugs pulling away, I got him into the car and I told him that I knew about the money he was really upset,

but he didn't have a choice as the scum after Bas had given him all my details and had told him that if he didn't get them at least the hundred euro that morning, that when I went up to collect him that I would get a bullet in the head. This wasn't a threat this was real life, they would shoot me in revenge for Bas thinking that he would care. They figured this would send a message out to all others, who owed them money. Irrespective of how small the amount would be.

That was an extremely long night and the next day was as bad .I cannot for safety reasons go into all that we had to do, but in order to stay safe we had to take him out immediately from the Youth-reach his dream school, but no point been in a dream school if you are a target to be hurt or worse. Sadly we were back to square one but what choice did we have. That weekend was extremely long now we had Bas crap and abuse at home, we had the worry of these other scum and we had no idea as to what else would follow. Late that afternoon I got a call from Jake on my mobile, he had gone out for a while with the kid that I hated Brian. When they were walking down the town they saw the people that were after him cruising around in a black car, he ran as fast as he could and was hiding out in an old house nearby.

I had only got off the phone from him when I got a call from one of the guys who had been involved in this situation with him, His number was blocked but as soon as I answered the phone it was clear who it was. He was so thick that even when I said his name his answer was so what you don't have my number the dumb fool had forgotten that I knew where he went to school, so it was going to be so easy to find his address. This piece of work told me that the next time I saw my son that he would be in pieces on a morgue table. Well I flipped I told him what I thought of him and what I would do to him, if he or his buddies so much as laid a finger

on the head of my son. Later that evening I was out at the shops and
another one of this dopey criminal buddies text me, it seemed that they all
had my mobile number by now and he was even thicker than his initial
dummy friend.

This one text me and the gob-shite had either not the brain cells to realize
or was just so strung up that he didn't remember, that once you send a text,
your phone number goes with it .Although I didn't have his name, I had
the number and the text that he sent, telling me that if I had sex with him
he would wipe out the debt. I did then what was my one and only option to
do, I gave his text and his number to the Detectives in the police and let
them deal with it.

The funny thing is I got lots of texts from Bas telling me that I settled
drug debts by having sex with the dealers, now that is weird as one I have
never ever touched drugs, I don't even drink alcohol. Bas turned me off
that for life, and I never ever told Bas that I had got those texts or what
was going on over him. So the only way that he knew what had been said
was by somebody telling him and I certainly never did, nobody knew and
after all it was him that they wanted, Jake was just the pawn to get to him.

Thankfully Jake was safe and managed to get away from the grip of
these people, but the danger that was around him was even closer to home
then you could imagine .As the saying goes keep your friends close and
your enemies even closer. At this stage Jake hardly slept, he would be up
all night waiting and listening for Bas to kick off, every night id go to bed
and wonder if I would even wake up the next morning and that is a
horrible feeling and one that I wouldn't wish on my worst enemy. Bas
drinking at this stage was unreal, he was literally drinking all day and all
night, he still drove his jeep, still went around as if he was the perfect dad
and the perfect husband, but our house was secluded it was in a town yes,
but in the rural area so nobody could really hear or see anything that went
on, it was a perfect setting for any type of abuser. One evening it had
started to get dark and Jake was still out it wasn't late, but the roads to the
house were extremely dangerous with no lights on them. He would
probably not even be seen by a car or van if it was just flying down the
roads as normal, so I rang him and went to collect him. When he got into
the car I knew that he had some drink on him and I was really angry, as I
hated to see any of the boys drink .It just reminded me of how their dad
started and having a grand-dad and a dad both alcoholics and my eldest

son also one, to me it was and is a genetic problem, as the coincidence of all three having the same addiction is too much to believe.

However I wasn't giving out to him, as I told him that we would just drive the car around the back and go on into the house, and if we saw Bas to just ignore him, that was the only way. Well Bas had different plans for us, as when we walked around the corner he had a can of cider in one hand, and a link chain in the other swinging it around at a height, that would hit whichever one of us came around that corner first.

Jake was the first around and I was right behind him, as he swung Jake ducked and he then dropped the chain and punched me in the Face. That was like red rag to a bull, as Jake just pushed him backwards and they fell onto the ground, it was crazy. I have no idea as to how Bas turned him around, but at this stage Bas was sitting on top of his 15 year old son, he was thrashing his head onto the tarmac. I was on top of Bas grabbing and twisting the chain around his neck, to try and pull him off as I didn't have the strength to physically restrain him. He was like ten men, the strength and the determination that he had, as far as I am concerned that night, was one where he wanted to kill our son and he would have found some way to have justified it.

With Jake out of the way then ,I was his easy target, he would just murder me probably in the night, when the boys all asleep and bring my body to the Dublin Mountains a favorite haunt of his and his criminal buddies. If they wanted to hide anything or anybody, as it is a needle in a hay stack and Id simply have just disappeared he would do the Joe o Reilly type interviews of course, but inside he would have been celebrating .Sometimes even the best plans don't go as planned, as out of nowhere ,somehow Jake got the strength to fight back. His face was swollen and bright red, he was having the life squeezed out of him. I was screaming, hysterical for ages and calling Rory who was in the house, there is no way that he didn't hear me he just chose not to. Jake turned Bas over and now he had the power, he had the control .I have no idea how a child who weighted at that time about 65 kilos, could take over control of a man, full of adrenalin and full of drink, who weighted easily 120 kilos more than his victim but he did It, and in the process he somehow managed to dislocate Bas shoulder. The scream from him to this day I can still hear in my head, did I do anything to help him, the answer is no. I got my son and my dogs who were also attacking Bas, despite them been his dogs they knew who was in the wrong and we walked into the house.

Rory went out to him and was telling me that I had to bring him to a hospital that he was crying and screaming in agony. Hell there was no way I was getting into a car with that man, and certainly not when he was still in such a rage ,that he would have killed me whilst driving the car, a perfect accident and a perfect alibi. At this stage I was a lot cuter than he realized and I knew that soon he would be gone thousands of miles away. I just had to bide my time.

He cried all around the house, all night at one stage I really felt sorry for him. I could see that his shoulder was dislocated as it was right down, but as soon as I was beginning to waiver and consider bringing him to the hospital, he started his verbal abuse again and , he didn't stop for ages. So I left him, I told him I had no pain killers and that I wasn't bringing him into any hospital .He couldn't drive as the car and jeep were manual so he was stuck. Eventually I fell asleep and when I woke in the morning there was no sign of him, around the house. I figured he had gotten a lift or a taxi to the hospital, so I rang the two main hospitals Mater and Beaumont as I knew he wouldn't go to any of the others. Low and behold he was in the Mater and had gotten the bus there. The poor thing had to have surgery to put his shoulder back into place, but even then he still couldn't tell the truth, he told them that he had fallen off his motor x bike in the field at the house. If they only knew the truth, he would have been arrested for child abuse attempted murder with his chain swinging and god knows what else, but as always he got away with it.

However this had proved to him that he could be taken down by his son so he in a way backed off for a bit, But like anybody who is an abuser, they cannot go long without that control, so after a few days when the pain had been eased enough by the alcohol mixed with the painkillers, he started mouthing off again. Adding fuel to the fire was the fact that one of his sisters who he had always been close to, but who he had been estranged from for a few years at this stage, my fault of course had been taken seriously ill in Spain where she lived.

As some family members flew over to her he couldn't as he hadn't answered a charge against him by Spanish police which is called a denuncia, and if he went anywhere in Spain with his passport, he would be arrested. So he couldn't go, again this was just another reason for him to freak and to feel justified in doing so. One thing that I did realize was that an abuser, an alcoholic and a controller, will always find any reason, any excuse to justify their actions, not to others but to themselves. All they need is one thing to happen, or to be said and then they will exaggerate it to the point of no return. That is why there is no guilt with an attacker, no conscience, as in their mind they are doing no wrong and in my opinion, that is the saddest part of all. Because of this personality trait they leave a trail of destruction that is carried on for years, in their children and in to the lives of any possible future grandchildren making them again the innocent victims.

Soon after his sister got ill, we got the news that she had died. I really felt so saddened by this, as at one stage in my life I was very close to her and I never found out as to why she turned against me. However having an evil sister in law who was one of his brothers wives that was known for causing trouble for her own benefits, didn't help. Somehow she always came out smelling of roses, as did her daughter, so family rift sort of made sense. I know that she filled Bas sister full of lies and bull about me. But that was who she was and sadly still is, but it is the only way in which she could feel important in life.

She was and is an Abuser of others, this now I clearly see, but over the many years that I was involved in Bas family, this woman who I call Cruella was nothing more than a trouble making witch, that thought the entire world should love her for been evil. Sadly many did as they were too scared to really tell her what they thought of her, personally I have no problems in doing that now. However for many years she bullied and abused me, by telling lies and spreading unfounded rumors. Jealousy really is an evil trait to have, Sadly in our world some people irrespective of how they look on the outside will always be ugly, as that ugliness generates from the inside out.

It is funny as I believe that now she is the best of buddies with Bas, as I am no longer in the family. What a relief. When his sisters funeral was organized the body was only to be viewed by the family. Bas freaked out at me, as I was apparently not family. Then the family where told that there was only a certain time frame for her body to be viewed du e to the fact that she sadly had not been embalmed correctly in Spain. It meant that for a short period all dislikes and bitchiness, would have to be put on hold. When I got ready at the house to go to see her body, Bas freaked, he went ballistic at me and started his shouting and insults .I was so worn out from him at this stage that I simply got into my car and drove to the funeral home.

If he didn't have the decency or the morals to see his own sister, than that was his problem not mine, although I knew I would be blamed for it. As I walked out from saying my goodbyes to her in the funeral home, he walked in. That look was in his eyes, and this time it stayed, this time it didn't go away. I prayed that he would stay with some of his family and let him be their problem for a night instead of mine. We went to the sister in law from hells house Cruella de Ville, my name for her, the place was packed. It is usual for a Irish Wake especially in a small town to have literally the entire town in the house to drink and remember the deceased.

I am not a 100 % sure if I can say that I fully agree with them, as it is really a big drinking session to say your good byes. But knowing what comes from those sessions, the upset, the emotions, and mix that with alcohol, it is a very dangerous element to have. I for one knew what would come of it, he could put the smiles on and try to be the nice man he wanted all to see him as, but those eyes those eyes didn't change, those eyes gave me the shakes. They have instilled a fear in me that will probably never go. Jake refused to go to the house or the wake, or indeed to the funeral. He didn't want to be anywhere near his dad, who by this stage he didn't even call him dad. He would say his dad was dead and that is a sad thing to hear any child say about a parent. But he was the wise one. At the wake I had wanted to go, it was really uncomfortable, as very few of the family spoke to me .I never knew why until about eighteen months ago, when I found out about his apparent daughter .They all knew her and they blamed me for him not been in her life, what fools they were. I didn't even know about her and she was the lucky one, not to have him in her life .At least one child was saved and possibly she is one of many, as with all his affairs god only knows how many other children he fathered and dumped. I stayed close to my boys at the funeral, as we all knew what would happen.

So we left the after party for want of a better word earlier than most and went home. The weird thing was that his oldest sister who had always hated me, and who knew nothing of my life with her brother for some reason just turned to me and told me that she knew what was going on between her brother and me. And that if he ever did anything to us again, that she would personally kill him. It is really amazing what drink makes people say, as I haven't heard from her since and that's over three years ago now.

The day after the funeral we had been booked on flights to Canada for two weeks. He had been offered a job there and they wanted to meet the family. The trip was a nightmare.as he was no different there than at home in Ireland. He hardly said a decent word to Jake and was always trying to get him to flare up into a fight, just so that he could blame him. It was pathetic to see a grown man, a dad who wants to fight his son the thought of it makes my blood boil and my stomach churn.

My plan was simple, that if we were going to be moving over there, that I would go along with it from the start but once I set foot over there that I would leave him. Then the kids and I would live totally separate lives from him. The sole reason that I wanted to do that there rather than in Ireland was very simple, at least there we had some protection from the law and if he did any of his abuse there that he did at home he would be behind bars. I only ever told Jake what my plan was as that way it was our secret.

We got back to Ireland and within ten days, he had to be gone again over to his new job, his new life. We had met some people over there that would help him with settling in .He was drinking like a fish now, if that was even possible but the excuse now was that he was leaving his kids and his dogs blah blah-blah. What little did he know that we couldn't wait till he went and especially Jake. The night before he went, he was in a bad mood, and we all knew that he was going to kick off. He was down in the stables drinking his cider and talking to Mark, he was always his favorite son and he always showed it especially to hurt Jake .He knew how close Jake and Mark, were so he would play one off the other if possible. At this stage I was sleeping on a futon mattress on the floor in the back living room there was no way that I was getting into a bed with him.

I heard him coming in the door of the house, then he started shouting that he wasn't going. I just ignored it none of his stuff was packed other than his passport and money that he borrowed from his brother .He had borrowed Euro 15.000 from one of his brothers who had sold his house. He made me go to my solicitors and get a letter of guarantee that I would repay this debt to his brother, from any inheritance that I got from my late dads estate. I had no choice as if not then with him going away. I knew he would make me regret it, so I got the letter. Recently my late father estate which had dwindled too little or nothing due to legal fees was resolved. I was held liable due to Irish Law to repay Euro 12.500 of this debt. Despite the fact that this debt was for the man who physically, mentally, verbally and emotionally abused me for over 20 years, and not forgetting that sex was rape to him. No under Irish law I had to pay this debt, it still makes me sick. Worse he ie Bas thinks it is great as he does not support his sons with me, and had me pay his bills.

But with not one thing ready for his trip and our escape from him just hours away, I never prayed so hard as I did that night that he would go. In a way my prayers were answered as at 0530 hours the next morning, I was kicked awake and been pushed at by him to pack his bag. Honestly I have never jumped out of bed so quickly as that day. He took his suitcases not knowing as to when if ever he would see his sons again, and he walked out the door, without so much as a goodbye, kiss my ass nothing he went and got into the car with Rory and off they went .At last we were free, at last Jake could now sleep at night and feel safe, in his own bed in his own house well for a short time at least. As you never know what is around the corner certainly not in our family and in our life.

About a week after he had gone, I called the police as I was so worried about my son hanging around with this kid Brian. I knew that he was bad news, and he had a dreadful reputation .But when Jake was with him he changed there was little that the police could do that night to help us. I will always remember it as it was a wet Monday evening but the officer took down all that I said and told me not to worry about Jake. That he would see his friend for what he was soon enough. What he said became a reality all too soon.

Now the deal with Jake was simple, because of where we lived and all that we had gone through, he had to be in by 9 pm. The roads were too dark to be walking, and I didn't want him just loitering around the streets, that's asking for trouble. So if he wasn't in, I would text his buddies to see if he was with them and usually he would be, then id either collect him or he would get a lift from one of his friends mams.

But this night was different and in my gut I knew that there was something wrong, they say that a mother always knows and you do. I called his mobile about a hundred times and no answer that wasn't him ,as he knew id panic no something was seriously wrong I text that thug Brian and asked if he knew where he was and he told me that he was busy and to fuck off .Now to send a text like that to your friends mam to me is not right ,so I text him back that if anything had happened to my son that I would kill him. I even told the police what I said to him later on that night.

This scumbag started to text me back and forth and still no answer to my sons phone. I didn't know whether to be worried and upset or angry at him, eventually I went into bed and left the doors open. I had thought that maybe he had drink on him or just his battery was dead in his phone, but that didn't make sense as the phone was ringing out.

About twenty minutes after I went to bed, a then friend of mine rang me and asked if Jake was okay. I told her what had been going on that night and what she proceeded to tell me changed our lives forever. A friend of her daughters had a business close to the beach in the town and he had got a call to say that the fire brigade were at his business. So thinking that there was a fire there he drove down, yet when he arrived he found lots of people standing around, The firemen were pumping the chest of somebody that somebody was my son Jake. He called my friend who called me, that was how I found out my son had died twice that night. I got Rory up out of bed and dressed, and we speeded down to the scene. All that was there was one police car and the same officer that I had spoken to about Brian only four nights earlier. When I told him what had been going on with the phones he told me that Brian was indeed there and that the reason I hadn't been called was that the thug, had not given my sons name or my phone number.

It later was discovered that at the time he was texting me abuse. My son was lying dying on the ground beside him, after having two cardiac arrests. Yet this insult for a human, as I don't see him as human could do was to text me calling me names, and telling me how busy he was. The only thing he was trying to do was to work out how to get out of the situation without been caught. My son had been coming home and Brian said that he wanted to show him something so like the fool he went with him. He brought him into what looked like an abandoned shed where there were a number of large Butane cylinders of gas. Brian then went over and stuck a nail into the top of one of them. When the gas came out he started to become very aggressive and was fighting and hitting out at my son. This was a planned attack by Brian. As nothing with this thing as he is not human to me, is ever by accident and always for his own personal gain.

Jake then ended up inhaling the gas that was in the closed room.
And started to fight back Brian but he dropped to the ground with his first Cardiac Arrest and was left lying there dying and to inhale the fumes in the room. Brian didn't even move him to the air or even initially call for

help as it was 35 minutes before any help was there how Jake is alive nobody knows except that it is a total miracle. We were given a police escort to Beaumont Hospital, I knew by the speed of the police car that it was bad that possibly my son wasn't coming home with me. Rory was arguing with me in the car telling me to calm down, that he was probably just drunk but you don't get a police escort for a teenager who is drunk, and they don't have to restart your heart either.

When I arrived at the hospital, it was like a scene from a movie all the staff just looked at me the pity in their eyes, it was very surreal. They ushered me into the family room, which had a small area in another room beside it where they would lay out his body. Rory was useless it was as if he was been taken away from something as he didn't even want to see his brother, I found out later it was cause he was or had been smoking weed, so he didn't care less what happened to any of us. But he also proved that the next morning, when he went to work as normal and left me with one son in a coma and two others at home with friends. The staff proceeded to tell me that when Jake had collapsed initially that he had two Cardiac Arrests and that the firemen had to use adrenalin and a defibrillator on his heart to restart it, But then he started to have uncontrollable seizures, they were so severe that they didn't think he would make it.

He had gone into a coma himself by the time the ambulance had arrived at the hospital. The hospital then decided to also insure that he was now in a induced medicated coma, as if not his brain would not have survived the amount of seizures that he was having and there severity. They ran all the usual toxicology tests and he had no drugs and no alcohol in his system simply the gas.

A doctor came in to talk to me and gave me the usual we have to wait and see story, but I had been around hospitals too much I needed the truth, no matter how bad it was. I had to know what I was dealing with, as that way I could try and get my head around it and find a way to help Jake. What he proceeded to tell me terrified me so much, that I actually hemorrhaged there and then, I totally destroyed my clothes with blood .Thankfully they were dark colored jeans and top so the doctor didn't see the state of them .But Bas nephew and his girlfriend were with me and she saw it, I suppose I had gone into my own type of shock.

The doctor told me that there were two scenarios for my son the best case scenario is that he would within the next 24 hours die as he was now on life support, and the second was that he would wake from the coma and that he would only ever move his eyes again. That he literally would be trapped in his own body, he wouldn't be able to do anything for himself, his speech and all movement would be lost. I told him that I would not put anybody through that torture and as much as I loved my son, I would turn the machine off if that was the way he would have to live his life. I couldn't imagine an energetic young man full of life very independent with lots of dreams and ambitions, now only able to move his eyes for possibly thirty or forty years. No that to me is a slow torture and I wouldn't allow it. I had no choice but to ring Bas and tell him, he was the last person that I wanted to see or even speak to but I felt he should know .Apparently his son didn't mean that much to him as he didn't even bother to come home to see him. Any other parent or sibling would fly across the world to try and help their child but not Bas, as with Jake gone then his life got a lot easier. I wouldn't speak to him after the initial call, I just let the ward staff talk to him as my sole priority was bringing my son home alive and as normal as I possibly could. He had spent his few years on this earth protecting and fighting for me, now it was my turn to fight for him and there wasn't anything or anybody that was going to step in my way.

When I went into see Jake it was like a scene from a movie there where doctors and nurses all just standing around the room looking at my son with such pity in their eyes, they didn't know what to say to me and couldn't even look me in the eyes. That was when reality hit home, that my son might never come home with me again. His eyes were taped shut, he was on a ventilator life support to help him breathe and to allow his brain to rest. One of the nurses came over to me to explain about all the machines and tubes that were on and around him, and to tell me not to be frightened by them, I wasn't in anyway upset by the machines. God id been in so many hospitals at this stage of my life, that they didn't bother me. But what was killing me was the fact, that when I spoke to my son lying on the bed dying, a single tear rolled out of his right eye down his face.

Now he was in a coma battling to live, yet somehow someway he would know that I was there and that one little sign was the only thing that made me at that stage determined to get my son back alive. To me, there was no way I was going to give up on him not now, not ever. He was unresponsive to the nurses, they would try and tickle his toes or get him to move his fingers, but nothing he was just lying there. Yet when I asked him to squeeze my fingers or wiggle his toes he managed to do it. At that stage the medical staff knew that for some reason, I was the only one getting a response from him so if anybody could bring him back it was me.

The machines can only do so much, but they told me that your hearing is the last thing to go when you are dying, so I never shut up yacking away to him. Telling him how much we loved him, and how there wasn't a hope in hell that I was going to let him die, that he had fought for me his entire life and never gave up, now I was doing the same for him. Jake was moved after hours to the ICU ward in the hospital. They told me that they didn't actually know how to treat his condition as although the hospital is the best neurological and poisons unit in Ireland, they had never dealt with the damage of Butane gas inhalation. This gas is unlike others, as it goes directly to the brain most will travel around the body to the lungs or heart, but butane starts to kill of brain cells that are called Neurons from the first second it is inside your body. That is the dangerous and scary thing about this as you can buy cans of it over the counter in small bottles or canisters for as little as Euro 2 in any store in Ireland.

Few stores have restrictions on it which is even more horrific as it is not law for them to do so. The only course of treatment that they could do was to flood his body with pure oxygen in the hope that it would help the brain to stay active. There were no drugs, no antidotes nothing but time and pure air been pumped into him and a lot of prayers. When he was moved to the Richmond ICU ward, the staff there where lovely, but the nurse looking after him told me that I was only allowed stay for 5 minutes and that I was to come back the next day
.
Well that was not going to happen, especially when she told me that in general the only way that patients leave that ward is on a trolley for the morgue. I was staying put and was not letting my son possibly die alone. She was arguing with me and ignoring what I had told her had happened in A & E .If I had to have a full blown argument in order to stay with my son, so that I could keep him alive, well that was what was bloody well going to happen. She was trying to get him to do the movements move the fingers, wiggle the toes but nothing. I knew that Jake could hear me, he had proved that downstairs so I said to her that he would move for me, she dismissed it and I simply said to her watch, I will get him to move and if I don't then I will not argue with you .I will stay in the waiting area and just come in and out every few minutes, but if I get him to respond then I am staying put for as long as it takes, without arguments from her, she agreed.

I am sure she thought that I didn't have a chance how wrong she was. So the bet started, I held his hand and spoke to him and asked him to squeeze my fingers and he did, he wiggled his toes and he lifted his leg, her face was one of shock, she said that she had never seen that happen before, and my answer to her was very simple you have never met or treated anybody like my son before Now in life that is why, if somebody says that we cannot do something, we simply say watch and learn. It might not be easy but can't is not a word that is in our vocabulary and never will be.

That night was I think one of the longest in my entire life, irrespective of anything that we had ever gone through this was like a nightmare that I couldn't wake up from. I sat by his side never left it, I was a total mess, my face was full of mascara, from crying, the make-up had vanished, my jeans were destroyed with blood from my constant hemorrhaging. But that is the way my body reacts when I am in total fear, but I held his hand. I got him to move his fingers and toes. I nagged and nagged him so much that he was going to wake up. Even if it was just to tell me to shut up.

The next morning he was still the same, unresponsive however he began to cough, now with a tube down his throat that is hard to do. The staff decided to try and take him off the life support as the longer that he was on it the less chance he had of ever coming out of the coma. However every time they would try and remove or touch the tube he would start to choke. There was foam coming from his mouth, his face was very red and he looked like he was simply about to choke in front of me.

I asked the doctor and nurse there that since he was calm and responsive for me that would they let me try. Now I had never done anything like this before, but if it meant that it would help Jake then I was going to at least try .I spoke to him first and told him what I was going do, he squeezed my fingers so I knew that this time he would let me take the tube out and take it out I did, .He didn't choke he coughed a little ,but no hysteria like before. The staff said that we had an incredible bond, that they had never seen before and that this was the first time that anything like this had ever happened in that ward.

As soon as the tube was out he sat up, he was like a lunatic, he was shouting and thrashing around the place .He then started to pull all the drips and the catheter out, he screamed with that one .I somehow managed to settle him down and he was brought to a private room in yet another ward. He was one of the very few who for want of a better word walked out of that ward as in general you don't go home from ICU not this particular one I was told so he was a miracle.

He started to come around and out of the coma fully he was very agitated, and as he had a phobia about hospitals the last place that he wanted to be was in one. All he wanted was to go home but he couldn't, not so soon, he simply couldn't comprehend how ill he still was. He remembered little at that time of the incident but in time remembered it all. He had every type of psychologists and doctor in with him, all in general asking same questions but none who had answers to mine. You see he had started to change, now id expected there to be changes in him especially considering the fact that they had told me how his brain probably wouldn't survive. But he looked fine he could move and talk perfectly, but there was something just not right, something that just was not there before. It took me a few days to figure it out and yet the hospital still did nothing.

I worked out that approximately every 15 -20 minutes he would go into a rage, he would be fucking and blinding at me and so angry and like a different person. Now these episodes would last for only about 5-10 minutes, but it was long enough in fact too long as he was extremely agitated. I spoke to the doctors and I told them what was happening they told me that it was normal .As after all there had clearly been some form of damage to the brain from the gas. The fact that they did not know exactly how long he had been lying on the ground in a coma after his initial cardiac arrest without oxygen was a concern for them. The length of time that he had lay there unconscious just simply inhaling the fumes was the issue, as the brain needs oxygen to survive.

They had no answers for my questions .I knew as much as they did about him now. What the future held nobody could say, and to this day the hospital has still let my son down. They like with his brother Rory never followed up, they never seemed to care if he was recovering or even still alive. No he was just another statistic but this time he was the survivor, thankfully. Shortly after he came home, he started to have seizures, now these were very unusual in the sense that his eyes would roll, his body would jerk but his head would bang against a wall or he would be standing thrashing himself around the room, I only last year found out from a pediatrician in the USA that this is called ballistic movements in a seizure and to some people he can look drunk or he can look as if he is high, when in fact he is seizing. These seizures unlike most other types of seizure would last for hours, he would seize for a few minutes then stop then start again this would go on for up to 5 hours, with intermittent breaks.

Eventually my Doctor managed to get us an appointment with a neurologist in Beaumont Hospital, but he was useless. He didn't believe me about the seizures and told me that it was impossible for them to happen for so long. Well as impossible as he may think that they were, the fact remained that they were happening and they did go on for that long and were the most horrific and terrifying type of seizure that I had ever seen,

The doctor told me to record him on the camcorder, the next time that it happened .Now with all due respect there was never a trigger point for them, so how the hell was I going to have a camera ready, and the last thing that I would be thinking of in a seizure is to record him. I had to stay with him, monitor him and talk to him they were my priorities not a bloody film. To this day that doctor has never got back to us with the results of the tests, his scans or his MRI so we are none the wiser as to what the problem is from the Irish Doctors. However the pediatrician in the United States was an amazing help to us.

In general after the seizure he wouldn't remember what had happened which is typical, he suffers from Raynaud's Syndrome which is bad circulation ,Hypoglycemia, what happened to Jake is called an Acquired Brain Injury as he was not born with it. But he is doing amazing. In general he has no issues and you would never know that he was near death so many times. But it is hard on him as to most he looks like a normal young man ,which in general he is, however if something happens that triggers an episode than people judge him rather than help him.

Thankfully the seizures are a lot more under control now and are basically non-existent. They only happen very seldom, but he knows when they are going to start, he has also found out that certain alcohol triggers them especially any type of cider, apple drinks or vodka so he just stays well away from them. Not that he drinks much at all and if he does it's very little. At least that's one good thing that came out of the abuse we lived through, he saw the full on destruction of alcohol .Not only within the family, but to the person abusing it as well, thankfully that is one learned behavior that I will not complain about.

We spent approximately six months after the coma with him been so ill and having non-stop medical problems, without the support of our Doctor and all in their clinic, I have no idea as to how we would have managed, without their care and attention as other than them we were on our own once again. Just after the six month period passed he had gone out for a few hours to one of his friend's houses and was due in at 6pm. It was in winter and the roads around us had no lights. However it was like a deja vu scenario, I spoke to him on the phone and he was on his way home, he never arrived, 30 minutes past, 40 minutes past and nothing. His phone was just ringing out, my gut told me that there was something wrong, when I couldn't contact him. I didn't know where he was, over an hour passed when his phone was eventually answered, but not by him, the infamous scum Brian picked it up.

Realizing that I would recognize his voice, he quickly told the two other thugs that he hangs around with to hang up saying that I would know it was him and he was right. I text his phone that if anything had happened Jake that he had better run, as I would this time kill him, id no idea still where he was if he was alive or dead or needed help. A few minutes later a kid answered Jakes phone and told me where he was. I was literally around the corner from him, as I flew around and who did I see running down the road only the three little scumbags themselves. Brian and his two scum buddies. Right now though I didn't have time to deal with them, I had to find Jake. The kid who answered his phone was waiting for us .Jake was in the back of a house that was been built, his face had been beaten up his lip all busted, his clothes filthy from the ground, and he was unconscious with eyes rolling. Panic set in, this is it I am going to lose him this time I thought. Mark somehow managed with a little help from me to carry him out to the car. I drove straight to the police station for help, but it was closed and nobody was around to help, it was a Sunday evening so it was a ghost town for the police. I rang the intercom to the next station but they couldn't help either all the police were busy. So with no other choice and in a panic, I rang the detective that I knew and within 10 minutes not only were all the local police that were now suddenly available at my house, so were the fire brigade and the ambulance crew. He was seizing again and in a big way, they thought that he would have to be intubated again. All the past fears came flooding back I was terrified. I told the police who it was and they dealt with it on that end .At the hospital we were back into the same bed in the same unit again and here we were trying to save his life, at just 16 years old he had gone through so much, life is so cruel.

They did toxicology tests he had no alcohol, he had no drugs, that they could find they had no idea as to what they were dealing with. Then I got a text from somebody in the town to say that the rumor was that these thugs had put Ketamine, the horse sedative in to his can of coca cola. According to the doctors that would make sense as it would give symptoms like he had but wouldn't show in the tests that they did. He was treated for same and a few hours later let home. The ketamine had crashed his blood sugars to only 0.3 away from a non-returnable diabetic coma, they nearly did it this time but once again he survived.

It turned out that they wanted to beat him up for the trouble they got into after the initial coma with the police. I had and have no hesitations in saying that I hung them all out to dry, I owed them nothing, Jake owed them nothing, they tried to kill him. So before they did the same to other parents children, I was going to open my mouth like many others should have long before, I wasn't going to wait for hindsight, I saw how that didn't work. So they knew that if they drugged him they would be able to beat him up and they did Sad though that this is what some kids are becoming in our world but their lives are going to be short, as living the way they do, their own bodies will give up on them and that is one loss that I am happy to say I will not ever shed a tear over.

Jake now wants to set up and run a program that will help other kids who are living a life of abuse, due to Domestic Violence. He has devised a unique plan that will also help them to understand and to respect firearms more in life, than sadly many do now. He still has his medical and neurological problems and probably always will. But like anybody with any serious injury or illness in their lives they have good days and you have bad days. But what many do not understand or realize in life, is that what happens in the brain either from an injury or through abuse, is hidden from the real world. Sadly it is also many times hidden from the victim in life until something brings it to their attention.

In general please always remember that just because somebody look's as you assume Normal, you do not know what goes on inside their head, nor what trauma they have endured in life. Ignorance to the plight of others has to change. I have seen people professionals think that somebody is drunk or high, when in actual fact they are having a seizure.

As the saying goes do not judge a book by its cover. Jake is the most determined and strong minded person I have ever known in life. I am so proud to say that he is my son and together we will succeed in living the lives that we should instead of simply existing, in order to hide the truth and protect the abuser who destroyed so much of our life to date. But that is the past, not our future.

CHAPTER 11

VEGAS- THE CHEF AND HIS PRODIGY

When people here you speak about Las Vegas they think that it is an amazing place that never sleeps and in some ways it is. It is a great city with some fantastic people in it .But it is also one of the loneliest states in the USA .It is known as the transient state as there are so many military families based there, that they stay in their own communities and they don't really mix with those outside of the military. This is understanable as they move so often it is easier for them this way.

However it is also a very sad state as the amount of Army Vets that you see living rough or begging at traffic lights would shock you. In actual fact you have to go to the town hall to get a license to beg at the lights .You see these former soldiers who fought for their country from a young age, sleeping on the sidewalks, no food, no shoes or torn clothes and a lot of them are even missing limbs. They are truly the forgotten soldiers and they are mere statistics in this very rich and very much a vibrant city.

Like all cities around the world there are areas that you don't want to go into, as you won't come out of them the same way unless your very lucky .But most people that you befriend there are actually from the west coast or the mid-west and they are very nice. The hotels and casinos are indescribable what you see on TV and in films is real, that is how they look and the craziest thing is that a queen sized room with every luxury you can imagine sells in these casinos from as little as USD 35 a night for the room. But they assume you will spend more in their casino hence making back more than the cost of the room. However if you have a few people in your party than your in heaven.

Summerlin is a beautiful but very rich part of Vegas, it is the safer of the areas to live in and is beside Red Rock Mountains and canyons It is literally in the foothills of same. I had come into a little money so Rory who was over in New York had told us to go over there for a holiday and to see if we liked it .At this stage he was working for this infamous Irish Chef, he had worked for him for a number of years in Ireland and had convinced me that all that had been written about him was untrue. The truth was that Rory was and is as bad as this chef .The two of them and one other man are like the three musketeers in the United States, they differ though as they don't take from the rich to give to the poor they take from the workers and especially the Chef and his silent partner with the money in NYC and they feed themselves and live the lives of luxury. While there workers go hungry and have their lives destroyed.

Anyway at first we met the chef and his wife from South Africa and their two kids and they were initially living in a house that was rented in Summerlin beside the Suncoast Hotel and Casino. We were brought over to the house and for Dinner although the tiny portions served, We ended up getting McDonalds on our way back to our hotel. They then moved into a mansion this is a house that you would see on MTV or Cribs it was out of this world. I had never ever seen anything like this, we are normal everyday people what you see is what you get and here we were been thrown into this world of flash and money and we had neither, but we went along with it initially.

The good thing about been here was that at this stage Bas did not know where we were, we had literally just got up and went during the night, it was the only way. He had been threatening for months that he was going to just arrive and take my youngest son who is now 12 years old and as he is Irish and the laws are so crap in Ireland, he could just arrive back

and try to take him from school without actually breaking the law. My son
to this day still lives under this threat and is in fear every moment he is
away from Jake and me. That is no way for any child to live life.

Everyday Jack would go to school with fear, he was so scared that he
wouldn't be coming home to me, it was horrible to see how this man who
was meant to be his dad and who should be looking out for his sons best
interests had him under such fear and he was making him physically sick.
The school were made aware of the situation as were the police, but it still
wouldn't protect Jack, as if Bas managed to get him then he would get him
out of the country. One way or another he has enough contacts to get
anything dodgy done, so a passport would be no problem to him. Jack
does not want to be around his dad or to speak to him, he doesn't live with
violence or aggression, he lives with fear of been taken yes, but he knows
that both Jake and I will die to protect him. He also knows that this is the
present not his future. Chef moved into this house in Red Rock Country
Club and had managed at this stage to have me working unofficially for
him. I was doing publicity and when he was then going to open his
restaurants in Vegas in the future, I was going to be head of admin. He
was going to sort out the visas etc. Sadly it was then that I started to see
what he was really like and I didn't like what I saw. His staff in New York
in the French cuisine restaurant had not been paid for over 8 weeks and
that included my son, yet chef was able to fly to and from Vegas at the
weekends which is very expensive, This was done in order to spend time
in the country club and to splash the cash, as nobody in Vegas queries
anybody carrying cash all you have to say is your here
to gamble.

We found a place to rent initially and it was in a small group of
villas in a gated community, it did not have the armed security
guard's that Chef had on his or the restrictions on who got passed
there check-point, no it was a normal area. In hindsight I now know why
he wanted that security, as it is very difficult even for police or
immigration to get past this guarded entrance without the home
owners been notified. That is the level of security that he had
and still has to this day. His two sons went to top private schools even
though they were very young they were paying over 20 k USD a year per
child just for Elementary school, and that didn't include any of the books,
or sports outside of school. I was totally shocked at the amount of money
that they spent on two very young children yet they had plastic plates in
the house as their dinner service, it made no sense to me at all.

A few weeks into our rental and his wife would want us over at hers all the time. Especially during the week, when he wasn't there. Jake however realized that it was just to have somebody else to watch the kids or to give her a break. The boys were about 5 and 8 in age and although only kids they had to be rocked to sleep at night and had their food cut up for them ,I had never seen children at this age so baby like it was not right, yet on the other hand they wanted for nothing. They had the latest I pads, I phones open accounts on the internet to buy games or whatever they wanted, to be honest I was in shock as to me that is abuse, as if they are been given all of this now at this age what would they be like when they were Teenagers, it is too scary to think about. The chef and his wife and boys were due to fly back to Ireland to get their green cards for permanent residency in the states. He had paid a top Irish lawyer who wasn't aware of his scams or lies over Euro 15 k just to get the application to this stage .Yet he would call her his favorite name a Jippo Cunt that was what he would always call the women men were Jippo Bastards, yet this woman was working for him. He got the name Jippo from Jewish people, as he would always say that they were very rich, but miserable bastards and he called them Jippo's he still does I am sure. To me this is a total insult to any and all Jewish people. I think that he was actually jealous of them and how successful many were in NYC were he failed. But that is my own personal opinion.

I had lent him a few thousand dollars at this stage as I was promised it would be paid back to me. Rory had been on the phone begging me as he said that he didn't have any money to do it, little did I know that my own son was scamming me but in hindsight I should have realized. I didn't have it to spare, but apparently his credit was going to be taken away, as he was late again the third month in a row for his car repayments so like the fool I was I lent it to him, .Not surprisingly I have never seen it since, he literally left us with nothing.

When Chef was away from NYC and in Vegas, I was getting calls from his staff that I had now made friends with in the New York restaurant. What they were telling me was scary and of course as always when money involved the chef was un-contactable. But there was a pattern to his scams as I found out. Not only that but he was linked in with another Irish man who has been living in New York for over 20 years. This man is originally from Finglas and thinks that now he has money that he also has power, and in some ways he is right. He owes over 1 Million in state taxes in New York alone, he owes over 600 people either money for wages or money for supplies that he received and never paid for and that was solely up until August 2012.

It has increased I am sure since then. So the secret scam artist and Thee Chef were a good partnership the only thing was that this other guy let us call him Tony was the silent partner. That was untill I started to get information on their rackets, Nobody knew the level of his involvement but it did make sense .I met this man once and once was enough, he was a slime ball, a small little squirt that thought he was Don Juan when all he was and is to this day is a down and out gangster. He lives in a mansion out in the Hamptons in New York and has anything and anybody that money can buy, hence one of the reasons as to why he has not been put behind bars for all their scams and frauds.

The restaurant that he financed for chef was on 72$_{nd}$ street in New York Westside, from the outside it looked like another stuffy, dark basement cafe but it was in fact a fine dining French cuisine menu, and in fairness the food got rave reviews initially that it deserved . The one thing that didn't though was the portions. The big man himself Chef insisted on small portions yet he wasn't getting hammered by the media reviews, Rory was. As always Chef had a fall guy and it is never him. This time it was my son. But as stupid as Chef thought that I was, as I am only a woman, I saw what he was doing and was determined to stop him once and for all.

So Chef let me in on one of his scams and from there, I was the only person in his career that I am aware to this date that has not only managed to get all the paper trail on them, but to have the inside knowledge that they do not want known.. He let me know what they were doing and how they were doing it. Now I started to gather more and more on him, as he could not be allowed to destroy so many innocent lives for his own financial gain. His wife from South Africa would pretend to be ignorant to his scams, but she was in them all and in actual fact was also scamming him in secret.

His first scam he did was one that apparently he has always Done and it works. He got me to set up lots of email addresses, I had to only do three from any one laptop or computer as otherwise it is too risky. When the email addresses were set up he would send me his reviews about the restaurant that he wanted on all of the tourist sites like Trip Advisor, and all the American ones. He would get me to put these comments up so as to boost the ratings of the restaurant and hence make him more money, now I never ever got a single cent from him, but that's him all over. But I do not want dirty money and that is all that Chef would ever have. Some of the reviews would be excellent and others would be complaining about one or two things, but he then would make himself out to look great by replying to the comments and offering a free meal or something of that sort. He was playing the entire American public and he had me helping him do it. When he would go home to Vegas at the weekend his manager also his wife would be doing the same and since she wasn't even in New York these sites had no idea as to how they were been conned.

Chef thought that I was his confidant, so I let him tell me all that he wanted to, as that way I was one step ahead of him, I now knew that all that was written about him in Ireland about not paying staff or suppliers and owing hundreds of thousands of euro to the revenue was totally true. Then doing the same in South Africa and having to flee due to the amount that they both owed and conned from people there. All that I had ever heard about this worm, I now realized was true. He had destroyed so many lives and was laughing all the way to the bank. My stomach would churn to even be in the same room as him, however if I wanted to report him then I had to get as much as possible in evidence so that it would stick this time.

His wife who had lived in Ireland for a while with their two boys in the K Club, would never stop telling me how much she hated Ireland and hated the people. Once something bad was written by the media about The Chef, that the entire country would gang up on him, and with every right. She is as bad as he is and their marriage is one of convenience. Despite what they say and the image they try to portray. I have been in their home many times, I have seen them together, I have seen their sleeping arrangements, this is simply a marriage of convenience and from conversations with the wife I know her reason.

You see with any African passport it is very difficult to travel around the world without a visa, as most countries demand one, But if she was to acquire an Irish passport not only could she travel around the world a lot more freely, she would always have it even if they divorced. Her ulterior motive was that she could also escape a city or country easily should the shit hit the fan with one of his scams. What infuriated me was that I found out all of this after she had told me with chef that I was to sign a form for her. This was to state that I was her friend for 10 years. Rory had been on the phone to me telling me that his job depended on it so I signed the form and only afterwards I found out the real reasons as to why she wanted a Irish Passport, I felt sick. I literally had only met her weeks before and had only spoken to her on the phone prior to that, but I was pressured and didn't have a choice as it would have backfired on Rory. I was also aware that she had stated that she had lived in Ireland longer than she had done .The Chefs sister in Ireland ,I think was also going to sign the form in her married name to say that she was also her friend for over ten years she played us all, and she got her passport.

When I found out the truth, I contacted the Dept of Foreign Affairs in Dublin and told them of the scam. There was no point in contacting the embassy in USA as they were friends with some of the consulates so that was a no go, Chef was high profile, he knew how to get anything that he wanted in the USA and who to get it from. I do not know if the passport was cancelled by the relevant Department, but I would hope that it was. As a woman who hates everything about Ireland, and it's people, and who would never live there again, in my opinion has absolutely no right to the privilege of a Irish Passport, irrespective of been married to an Irish Citizen. But this was just another scam in their lives and another thing that they felt entitled to.

When Chef was back in Ireland for his meeting with immigration in the USA Embassy. He had his solicitors organize this for an appointment in Belfast, he thought it would be easier up there than in Dublin. He failed to tell them the truth though at the interview. You see he had hired a top immigration lawyer in Ireland but had lied to her also, he didn't care and doesn't care if her reputation is slandered or dragged into his scams, all he cares about is that he got what he wanted. But I cannot say her name as she is just another victim of this man and his scams.

The wife prior to them leaving Vegas for Dublin ,then up to Donegal and Belfast, was trying to remember what she had put on old forms as she hadn't kept copies of everything. This is hard as they don't like paper trails and hate if there is one on them, she wasn't sure what she had put down about his court cases in the past or his extradition to Ireland some years ago or the truth about his original marriage .She was in a panic but clearly she said the right things as The Chef ,his wife and two sons flew back to Vegas a month later with their green cards and this made him even more dangerous.

What a lot of people don't know is that chef had about 15-20 years ago married an American girl. I won't put her full name down but her first name was Jennifer and thankfully she has a new life away from him. However whether or not she was aware at the time and I very much doubt it, but chef only married her for a social security number and therefor a legal visa. She didn't give him his divorce as quick as he wanted but in the end he divorced her. Then he went on to marry the African beauty queen who had worked with him in her home country before they ripped so many off and had to flee. After all what man doesn't want arm candy, she also secured her future by giving him two kids and she would now also be armed with an Irish passport, and an American visa. As sad as it sounds in some ways you could say that crime does pay as it has in their case.

Chef and his wife lead basically separate lives, if he isn't in New York or LA he is globetrotting around the world, as a consultant. He does this whilst claiming to be broke all of the time, but what these innocent hotels and restaurants don't realize is that they are setting themselves up to be the next target. He sleeps in the master bedroom when in Vegas and she sleeps in with the boys, in all the time that I knew them, I never ever saw a glimmer of love or affection, they were just like business partners or partners in crime which is what they are. When they were in Ireland getting their passports for the wife and two boys and their visas for all the family they left the restaurant in New York in a dreadful state. Staff members were losing their homes, their credit which in the USA is so important and the sole reason was that Chef and Tony wouldn't pay them their wages. The till in the restaurant never had money in it solely as every morning Tony would walk in and empty it, then walk out but instead of it going into the business account it went into his personal one.

He would invoice the restaurant for consulting and administration fees, when he did nothing there except take the money, Of course Chef would always come up with an excuse as to why there was no wages for the staff, or why the supplier wasn't paid he had an excuse for everything and could charm his way out of any situation. I saw with my own two eyes and how very convincing he could be at that. He even had Rory pay suppliers out of his own personal account in order to insure that the restaurant was open that night, yet he would never get repaid this money. It was so sad to see how Rory was so brainwashed by these gangsters, he never argued about them not repaying the money, he just went along with it.

As Chef had spent time in an American jail before he was deported to Ireland to answer charges of theft. Which again he got away with, he had made friends with some of the old school Italian Mafia guys that he cooked dinner for when they were behind bars, so this to him meant that he was protected by the mafia .They simply got a free meal off him, they owed him nothing even if he thought that they did. One of his scams was a simple one and if I know him he is still running it to this day, What he would do is to write out a check to a supplier for supplies that they had received and or wages to staff but neither he or Tony would sign the checks, no they would get Rory or somebody else who was not an authorized signatory to sign the checks, knowing that when they were presented to the bank that they would be unpaid. Hence allowing them more time without paying, this they would do on a regular basis .Eventually the banks put blocks on their accounts, but it didn't top them, all that they did was to open accounts in a different bank.

If suppliers threatened them with court, they told them to go ahead, the same was said to staff as they knew that it would cost these victims more to go to court than they had, and also more than it was worth if they won. So simply their reply to this problem was get a new supplier and then fire the staff who only wanted their wages .At one stage he also had Rory who was sharing his apartment with him and who was paying for this out of his wages he had him sleep on the floor on a blow up bed, the reason well he had hired all the furniture in the apartment and as he was not there that much he had them collect it and told Rory that it had been repossessed. But that was a lie, he told them that he wasn't there so they could collect it .He had played the one person who had stood by him no matter what. It was impossible to get Rory to go against chef he was brainwashed so much by his power, his respect and his way of life always flashing the cash, sadly he was now not only his prodigy but he was his twin.

He knew all about the scams all about the money laundering, the not paying staff, he was as bad as them in my mind as he stayed with them and it made me sick. During the time that chef was sorting out all his paperwork in Ireland, the staff had basically walked out of the restaurant on 72_{nd} street. They couldn't afford to work there, and they thought that if they closed it for a day or two perhaps Tony, who was still in New York running his group of Irish Bars would pay them at least some of what they were owed. This went on for weeks and some staff got some money, but nobody was ever paid the full amount.

One of the chefs was an amazing girl called Brenda, with a name like that you would think she was Irish, but she was from Argentina in South America, her pastry and desert skills were out of this world. When she went to work for chef he had told her that he would work with her attorney in order to get her visa, so that she could stay in the United States. Months past and she was forever asking him and Rory to send the relevant documents to her attorney as she had paid him thousands of USD, this was literally all that she had, and they had done nothing. The day before her temporary visa expired Chef told her that he wouldn't have the paperwork ready, she had wasted thousands of dollars, put her life on hold had worked for little or no wages had produced deserts that customers raved about and brought in a lot of revenue to the restaurant.

Yet as usual she was dispensable and just dumped .My heart went out to her, if I could have helped her ,I would have as she didn't deserve this treatment, yet she had to fly home the next day broke all cause she worked for Chef, Rory and Tony .A lot of staff started to now get really pissed off, as chef was in Ireland, Tony was nowhere to be found and Rory himself hadn't been paid, So the staff literally walked out, the restaurant had to close down and once again chef insured that he owed thousands of dollars to so many innocent people, their only crime working for him or supplying him.

To say that I was infuriated is an understatement. I still had not got my money back and he was having a holiday for over a month, yet he did it on everybody else's money as usual. So one night I was speaking to a former member of staff and in order to ensure their safety I won't disclose anything about them. However they like me wanted to stop chef and to try to get all the money that was owed to everybody. So with keys that they legally had for the restaurant they went down to the basement where the tiny office, computer and files were. What was found didn't surprise me, but I was still amazed, however we managed to uncover a lot of information on how the scams were done and what they did. The Dept of Labor in New York was well aware of not only Chef but Tony .The amount of complaints that had been filed against them was unreal yet they ignored them. One of their scams was to photocopy a potential staff members ID whether that be passport or driver license and also their social security number. Now in the USA you need a social number for everything so these were gold, of course the person handing over the information had no idea as to what was going on. But Chef and Tony would then give these numbers to use to illegal staff in their bars and restaurants. Unbelievable at one point Chef even asked me to give him my late dad's social security number for Rory I refused of course.

Nothing is done without a fee as far as Chef and Tony are concerned, I have no idea as to how much they charged these workers that they sold the above to, but I assume knowing them they would have to work a few weeks for free .He would also have dummy invoices from Tony and himself for consulting fees at the restaurant or bars. This would then legitimately give them the reason to take money from the business. Chef would arrive into Vegas at the weekend pretending to all that he was broke but he wasn't you don't go and spend time lounging around the pool in the country club with no money. What would happen with the money when he brought it to Vegas, is that the wife would put this money onto a lot of different pre-paid credit cards. This way they were guaranteed no names on them and no paper trail, a perfect way to launder money and defraud the IRS in the process.

A certain amount of money would be put into bank accounts in her maiden name, mainly he thought that this was the intelligent thing to do as no paper-trail to him. But she told me that she was putting the money away in her name so that once she had the visas, if shit hit the fan she was going back to South Africa to live. Since neither he or Tony were down as the restaurant owners they thought that they could get away with anything and in theory they have for many years. They had company names that all had limited liability for something as small as Euro 1 so they didn't care they were covered. Now considering that they left over a million ram in debt in South Africa and abandoned their house with kid's toys and pictures it's not somewhere that Chef will want to go. So she knows that she will have a good life with his money. The amount of scams that he runs amazes me, as he hasn't cooked in a kitchen himself in over 9 years, he shouts and he abuses the chefs that do work for him yet he takes the praise for all their hard work .When customers comment on the presentation or quality of the food he takes these compliments, as if he has presented the plates. however if there is a complaint well then it has nothing to do with him. He simply storms into the relevant kitchen demoralizes all the staff and shouts at them with no respect at all, and the sad thing is that all he has done is to dictate. Hitler will never be dead when he is around that is for sure.

By now I knew that he was total thrash, I had evidence of frauds that involved the American Dept of Labor, IRS, Immigration Fraud, Bank Scams and Frauds, Dept Health & Safety .In the restaurant in New York he had a cat in which was hidden at times in the basement. He had Rory go and find him one day as its sole purpose was to kill rats that ran across the floor under the tables in the restaurant .He called the cat killer, as on the previous evening before Killer arrived, unknown to customers three rats were seen by staff running across the dining room floor .Hence the cat to kill the rats as better and cheaper than pest control.

At this stage I told Rory what I knew, I told him on the phone that I had now copies of all the paper work that proved all the scams of chef and Tony. He freaked at me told me, that I was ruining his career, that I was taking away his life, and all he had worked for. I didn't recognize him anymore, as all he was interested in was money, drink, drugs, highlife but that comes at a cost .I told him that I was going to go public, if this was not sorted immediately. I wanted my money back which I was in dire straits for and all the staff where to be paid.

The following day Tony went to the restaurant whilst it was closed but there was somebody who saw him, anyway he wiped the computer of all information, the hard drive was emptied and he also shredded all of the paper trail that I already had. This from my understanding meant that they thought that they were one step ahead of me, when in fact all of the paper trail had been copied the night before and I had received same in attachments on emails .I had the paper trail that they so wanted hidden, it was now on no computer but stored safely. And another person also now had a copy so even if they managed to get my copy they wouldn't find the other one. Chef was on the phone to me telling me that this situation was all Tony's. Now I knew that the two of them were in it together and that up until now nobody in the public knew of their connection, it was like a secret that had to be kept. I told them that I was going to put it up on Facebook and that id let the entire world see what they were up to, I was begged not to post it, and told that my money would be repaid, that the staff would be sorted within the next 24 hours. So I left it for that period and nothing was done, so I set up a Facebook page called Sarahjayne and my profile was of a little rat playing a trumpet I thought it was very fitting.

Ballistic is not the word for it, Chef went crazy threatening me, freaking and shouting at me, and telling me that I would regret going up against him and Tony. Here he was threatening the mom of his top chef, yet he didn't think twice about the abuse he gave me, but all he did was to infuriate me. I knew that he was abusing all these people and having lived with the abuse from Bas for so many years, I wasn't going to take this.

The Facebook page went viral the amount of people that sent me information, that I didn't know about his scams was unreal. So many people around the world had tried and failed to get their money and their lives back, that he stole from them, and all in general failed. He was always one step ahead of the posse, had the best lawyers that money could buy, the best dressed in court and the charm to match, he was a player thru and thru. The sad thing was that he knew about some of the abuse not all that, I had gone through, yet he thought that it was okay to threaten me, no this time I wasn't taking it.

One night I logged onto my email and saw that I had a lot of people that had accepted my friend request. Now I knew that these were already my friends and that I had no reason to send them a new request, but what I saw and found out to this day makes me sick to the core. Chef along with Rory as the information was too detailed, too personalized set up a false Facebook page about me. They somehow linked it into my own personal page and they sent all my friends requests. They put up on the page our address our exact location and phone number.

But worse they also put my profile pic of one of me holding my deceased daughters name plaque. I shook with anger and upset, I knew that they were low but to bring in a little innocent deceased angel into their sordid and criminal acts was disgusting, Jake was fit to kill he wanted to go to confront the chefs wife but that is what they wanted, no we would get them some other way.

At this stage we had met through social circles a man who was working for a law agency in Vegas and he was not the type that would sit back and ignore this. He was used to dealing with scum of this caliber. So I gave him the access codes to my account and my email and he within minutes had the page taken down. We still had the proof though, as the emails for the page had all been sent to my own email address, so even with the page itself gone. We had the evidence and it was been tracked back to these people

.

Not only now had they put me and my kids at risk as Bas would have seen our address, they actually rang him and gave him our details, that is how low they were willing to stoop. But they wanted what I had on them, one way or the other. We decided there and then that we would have to move as it was too dangerous, with Bas knowing where we were .Yes we had protection but not enough that would stop him. Now Bas would do anything to have me killed, he would be more than happy to pay for another person to do it, Yes he would enjoy the thrill himself but with a good alibi, and me still dead. All his dreams would have come through. We had no idea if those that broke in were connected to Bas and just made it look like a burglary to distract us or if they were to do with the Chef. But we knew that the Chef had been in contact with Bas in Canada telling him that they had to shut me up.

Neither cared who got me murdered first and they still don't, as once I am dead then they are free to do what they want without fear of been caught and been held accountable for their actions,
A few hours afterwards we went out, when we returned to the house we noticed that there had been somebody in the house We rang the official we knew and also the cops, they had gotten in from the rear of the house through a window, that although was alarmed the sensor didn't work .It was the only one like this yet they knew, so the only way was for somebody inside to have known and that had to be down to Bas and the Chef. I told the police officer that I feared it was either Bas or somebody that had hired to find us, as he had been on the cell threatening me that he was coming to Vegas to get me, and sort me for once and for all and that he was planning to take Jack. This information along with the details on the Chef were all filed by the officer. Also at this stage the friend in law now had the information on them. Although most of their crimes were based out of state in New York, they were also setting up Vegas and now Orange County in California.

They were planning on opening a few new restaurants in Vegas, so at least this way the authorities would be aware of him and his plans and hopefully stop them before they started. At this stage we packed what we could and loaded up the car we went and stayed in a hotel that night. The next morning we met our friend and a colleague of his and they both wanted to help us but to put us into protection, as what I had already told them they were able to verify. So they knew that I was telling them the truth, however as we had an Irish passport and there were agreements between the countries they couldn't put us into protective custody. As we could go home to Ireland they were as frustrated as we were and we didn't know what to do.

I then started to get the abusive and threatening phone calls from Bas .He knew all that was going on ,he knew where we were and he told me how he was on his way to the state ,or somebody for him was and that it would all be over soon. Jake took the phone off me and told Bas what he thought of him, but both Jake and I both knew that the threat from Bas was very real, and that he would do anything in this world to have me dead. We went downtown and the office of the agency was closed. We called 911 and officers arrived. We told them our situation and our fears, we were stuck with no money, no were to sleep and no idea as to who or how many were after us .A wonderful officer J I could not say her name here ,but she told me to wait in the car we had, she came back with burgers and fries for us all with drinks, Her kindness restored our faith in humanity. She told us about a hostel for victims of Domestic Violence but as Jake was then 17 he would have to go to a homeless shelter. That was not ever going to happen so we stayed in the car together. If Bas was going to find me then he would find us together They suggested that until we got home that we would go to a small town in middle of nowhere .That way at least if somebody came looking for us we would have notice as in a small community we would be safer. So my hair was all chopped off, I cried when I saw it, Jake at this stage had a beard so he left it on and we decided to get some form of weapons for protection. In Vegas it is not illegal to carry a weapon once it is on view however in order to carry a concealed weapon you need a license So Jake got armed and I had a weapon on me at all times.

However as if it wasn't bad enough that we had been broken into the previous day, when we went back to the house to get more belongings, and to feed their pets but we sensed that something was wrong. The house looked fine, yet the alarm that had been put on was now switched off at the controller .So somebody had been in or was still in the house that knew the code. Jake locked Jack in the car gave him a mobile and told him to stay hidden, that if one of us didn't come out to get him in 5 minutes that he was to ring 911 and not to open the door to anybody .When we went upstairs, we could see that the master bedroom had been thrashed all the drawers had been opened papers were all over the place and it was like a tornado had hit the room.

The scariest of things was that in Jacks room where Jake sometimes slept, to keep us all in the same area, when the threats started was smashed on his side and both their wardrobes and bedrooms searched ,but still how did they get in. Standing in the en-suite it sounded very noisy more so than usual you could clearly hear all the passing traffic. When Jake pulled back the blind he saw that the window was still open a little and the screen had been taken off, but the blind was back down clearly whoever it was intended on coming back ,to either search more or to harm us and we were not waiting around.

We rang our friend again and cops arrived in unmarked car within minutes, he took all the details and gave us a case number. At this stage we were in danger not only from Bas as he now knew where we were, the chef and Tony who wanted what we had and then the possibility of a gang that the Chef and Rory had seriously pissed off in NYC. Some months prior to this in Vegas, an incident that had occurred in New York, that I had only been made aware of, and now we were also considering along with the police authorities if this also was related to the break in. We had the joint worry of Bas finding us and getting rid of me, then we had the Chef, his buddies and now possibly a Mexican gang, how the hell where we going to get away from them all.

MS 13 is one of the world's most notorious gangs and you don't ever get involved with them or go against them, I hadn't but Chef and Rory had, and in doing so I had recently found out nearly had poor Jake killed whilst he was with Rory for a short while in NYC. When Jake told me what happened and then I logged on to Rory Email ac which I still had the passwords for ,and saw what Chef and Rory had done I was so angry that I was flipping out . They had jeopardized every single family member belonging to both of them, and to anybody that worked or supported them and their crimes

This incident happened a few months prior to me even going over, and all had been sworn to secrecy about it .Not by the police, no by Chef and Tony. But I now knew why as he knew I would go absolutely crazy if I found out the truth .Yet the truth when I did find it out was worse than I could have imagined ,at this stage I knew that neither Rory my son or Thee Chef had any morals or self- respect and certainly none towards anybody that they came into contact with.

A few months prior to me untangling their webs of deceit there was an incident that had happened in the restaurant, on 72$_{nd}$ street .This incident and the actions of The Chef not only risked the life of Jake and Rory but also mine and Jacks .Who the hell did this man really think he was .What had happened reads like a script, but it is the sad reality of what happens to anybody who stands up to the chef, his prodigy and or Tony. In general Chef would prefer to hire a lot of Mexicans as he knew they were hard workers. He would employ a lot of illegal workers actually nearly all illegal for two reasons. The first was that they wouldn't complain or go to the Labor department if they didn't get paid or their basic rights, and the second been illegal they would do the jobs that nobody else would dream of .It was like the times of slave labor in the South of America, yet this was happening in everyday life in New York City. One man in particular was called Meco as he was from Mexico. Anyway after weeks of looking for his money for working on his hands and knees ,he had to scrub the floor with a nail brush. Every morning he would have to clean up the vomit that had been left during the night by revellers going home after having too much to drink. The jobs that were revolting and demoralizing this man was forced to do by the Chef and Rory, he was as bad as the chef in the way he spoke to this man. One day in the restaurant. Chef wasn't there he very seldom was, but Rory was as was Jake and Brenda and a few others. Meco started to freak and threw a chair through the window, the police were called and he was arrested. Now what he did was wrong yes , I don't agree with what he did, however I do understand as to the reason he had for doing it.

He was simply looking for the money he was entitled to and had worked his ass off, for over 8 weeks for and yet had still not seen a cent of it. There was always an excuse, always a reason and because they knew his circumstances they all played this poor man. He had wanted to send it home to his family in Mexico they were relying on it. That was the sole reason why he was in the USA so that he could provide for those he loved in his home Country all that this man did was work his guts out. That night Rory had a girl in the apartment that he shared with chef in the famous Trump Tower as chef was in Vegas .He told Jake who was only there for a few days to go to McDonalds for a while, .As he did, now he was from behind very similar to Rory, three guys shouted at him Hey Chef and he turned and said yes and they beat the crap out of him, they stole his jewelry, his trainers they tried to burn his face with an aerosol and lighter. Their first kick was to his lower back as they knew Rory was recovering from a broken back, so it was a targeted attack.

They told him that the bail for Meco of USD 2000 had to be paid or they would be back. Now Jake is not one to scare easily, but this shook him up badly. When he managed to stumble back to the apartment to Rory he wouldn't let him in, as he was busy with the girl, he had to get the doorman to let him in, it really showed him Rory's true colors hadn't changed. He was petrified as these weren't just three street thugs these were gang members of one of the world's most notorious gangs the Mexican MS 13.They had the tattoos all over their necks and arms as strong as he was he hadn't a hope in hell against them. And the Chef and Rory's answer was simple you can't go to the police it will only get you into trouble, in fact it was them that they were covering not poor Jake. Them and their scams. In time I found out that Chef had actually had members of staff make statements to the police about the incident in the restaurant. However the statements they made were all based on lies, they made false affidavits, as in order to keep their job what Chef and Tony wants Chef and Tony get. This meant that although the man who smashed the window was wrong ,he was now going to get a jail time .You don't lie about any crime and most certainly not against a gang member like MS 13 ,but Chef, Tony and his prodigy think they are invincible.

When I heard this I contacted the District Attorney's office in New York and left many messages .As this man did deserve punishment for the window, a fine, or something but not his life ruined over the lies of the Chef, Tony, Rory, just for their own satisfaction .Yet again they won and the poor man was brought to court and as far as I know went to jail and as he was illegal would be extradited after sentence, as is the norm in the states. To this day this particular incident makes me sick. What this Chef, Tony and Rory did not only endangered the staff who were forced to make the false affidavits, it endangered all our families, as MS 13 don't let you away with this type of abuse. They knew the name of the chefs their and all the staff, and anybody who was involved in this situation was at risk.

Now Vegas has a high concentration of MS 13 members and whether it was them or it was to do with The Chef, Tony or Bas, we will never know but it was too dangerous for us to stay in that house, and in that area, there was no way after escaping our life with Bas that we were going to now loose it because of this Chef, Tony and Rory. For a few days we stayed in hotels they thankfully were not too expensive there and we had a rental car. What we didn't pawn, we sold. We had to get money fast and that was the only way. Where to go now, we were alone yes, we had the contacts for the law agencies but their hands were tied. We didn't have enough money to fly home, so we had to go into hiding on our own and hope that we would make it. It was either a small town in the lower 49 or go to where Jake had always dreamed of Alaska, so we figured we would be safe there. We had been in the heat of Vegas, most days 110 degrees now we were going to the unknown and we really were alone. We missed our first flight and we thought that we would be stuck there as we were late but we had got lost within the airport as it was so big, anyway we got a later flight and flew to Seattle and from there on a connection. This alone had us take three trains within the airport and run to catch the door of the flight as there had been literally a 30 min connection. Ive no idea as to how we made it but we did.

When we arrived into Anchorage it was all white, it was covered in snow and the cold was unreal we were frozen solid. I had booked us in to what looked like an okay hotel close to the airport and they did come to collect us at the airport. However when we arrived and checked into our room, we immediately checked right back out. The beds were dirty, the pillows had hair on them, and the towels had been used to wipe an asshole or that's what it looked like, The manager came up and smelt the sheets and said that they were clean, it was just stains that had been washed in. But that they were fresh on the bed, and the hairs must be from the tumble dryer .Well we waited in the lobby all night, till the next morning and we had no idea as to where we were even heading but fate stepped in.

Jake was outside having a smoke and was speaking to native lady who told him about the towns that he should go to and where was the nicest. So we got a taxi that morning to a town called Wasilla, it was small compared to Anchorage still as cold but had everything in it, We stayed in a apart/hotel and had a full kitchen in the room and it was spotless. We ended up becoming good friends with a lady who worked there called Chris who really was a god send to us at a later stage. The native lady had told us about a little town called Talkeetna which was a train ride away or about 90 minutes in the car, so with no car we said we would get the train .However it only goes there once a week so we had to wait till the Saturday morning, it was a magical journey, the scenery, the countryside, it was just indescribable. And for Jake who hated leaving Ireland to say that he was now home and would never leave, it was amazing. But I knew how he felt this place was special, it may be remote but it was perfect or so we thought, but for now it was our safe zone.

When the train pulled into the town, the main street and the train station are basically all the one, it was so cold and icy yet the people where so welcoming .It was a kindness that we had never seen or experienced before, we were met at the train by a cab that brought us the five min drive to the chalet that we would stay in for a few days .It let us get our feet on the ground and to settle in. After that we were moving a bit but it was still in the same area, on the first day there Jake got a job without pay, but he just wanted to learn and to spend time around the animals, his voluntary work thought him so much about mushing, he was always great with animals and knew husky dogs but he hadn't a clue about mushing but he loved it and it is something that will stay with him for life.

It was only temporary as for the time of year, but it was great experience for him. After a short while we rented a cabin for a week but it was so basic that we couldn't stay there .Not only was the toilet in the living room and kitchen but if you were walking down the stairs you could not only look into the toilet, but the door was only a half door so you could hear whoever was in there as well it wasn't exactly the best of situations. Add onto that the water pump that was like a tractor engine and the heating boiler all in the same vicinity of the only toilet, this was a noisy house and very hard to sleep in.

We had a loft that we shared with our three mattresses but it did for the week till we found another place. I got a call about a cabin that was less expensive than this one yet was ten times the size had proper rooms and bedrooms and only around the corner. In this area as it is so remote it is hard to find anything like this, so we jumped at the chance to view it. Perfect ,yes it was filthy and needed lots of TLC but it would suit us and it had a wood burner, so we could keep the house warm with just wood. I got some part time work cleaning log cabins that were used for weekend holiday rentals and as I could not work for money, the lady gave us bed clothes and linen for the house, along with Coffee Maker etc. It was perfect as at least we got what we needed and it was much appreciated.

About this time I got the contact details for a lady who had a coffee shop in the town, but she was closed for the season as she was too busy to run it, I rang her and agreed to meet her with the option to rent the shop but to work it at weekends initially to see how it went, nobody knew about this meeting as we had kept it very quiet or so we thought. Two days later I got a text on my mobile from Bas asking me how the restaurant business was going .Now the only thing close to a restaurant that I had been checking out was the coffee shop, this scared the hell out of me was he here, had he found us and how the hell did he know. We had no answers to our questions and we were back now to looking over our shoulders. Two nights later whether it was to do with him or the chef or just a coincidence we will never know but it made us petrified.

Jack had been climbing a tree and had fallen off it, but it was very clear that he had broken his wrist however having no car and been so remote there was very little we could do .Somehow we had to get to the hospital in Wasilla, he was in agony and even with painkillers I wouldn't be able to stabilize him. Thankfully a friend Kathy said that she would drive us in, wait and bring us home she was such a godsend, as otherwise we would have had to wait till Monday. The hospital was amazing and they took Jack in very quickly he was screaming in agony even with painkillers so they gave him some very strong narcotics to relax him and they brought the x-ray machine to him. After about 30 minutes he was dopey enough for them to do the x-ray and they found that he had broken the bones on both sides of his wrist which explained the pain. He had never broken anything in his life so this was his first.

Whilst there Jake who was at home lighting the wood stove and watching a movie on the laptop, as we didn't have a TV, he rang me in a panic the modular home directly across from our house blew up. There were flames everywhere, now there had already been a horrific fire down the town on Halloween night at 2am or something like that but we were in bed, didn't even know about it till later next day. But this was right beside us, I told him to stay away but as a teenager they don't listen he rang the fire service and he ran out to help. He was filming it on his I phone when he saw one of the firemen had gotten stuck so he dropped it to the ground and just ran into the fire and helped him out. He then helped with other neighbors to put the flames out, apparently it had they thought been a met lab as it was all boarded up at the front but for an explosion like that it made sense.

The next evening we were at the decking at the back of the house Jack was inside as he was in pain and Jake was looking for his axe so that he could cut some wood for us, there was a glow at the side of the house which looked yellow or orange we didn't know what it was, until we ran around. I went through the house and Jake went around the side .Then we saw that the shed of the house beside us was now on fire .he wood was very dry and the flames were shooting over towards our house. We got Jack out and we rang for help ,I took all the fire extinguishers out of the house and between them we used them all but to no avail .It took hours before the fire subsided and at this stage everybody was scared ,this was a sleepy town these things didn't happen. Yet here were three unexplained fires in abandoned buildings in a few weeks.

We were told that there was a guy seen around the town earlier that day, that was actually banned from the town and that he had a grievance with at least the two houses beside ours over drugs and he had just been released recently from prison it all seemed such a big coincidence, Yet it got us to worry, as they were so close to our home, the text message that we got had this something to do with the Chef / Tony or with Bas we didn't know or worse still MS 13.

Had we been watched, even now we got scared and paranoid we then rang our contact in Vegas and he told us to get the hell out of there fast, no delays, take what we could and to leave. Too many things had been happening around us and all of them to cause us upset and distress so that night we packed our bags .We put as much as possible into them and left what we couldn't take, but we had a problem the next train wasn't for a week, we had very little money and we had no transport we were stuck literally sitting ducks. Remembering that Chris in Wasilla had kindly said that if we needed anything to call her, so we decided that we would try. I explained to her what had happened and she told me that she would drive up for us but that there was a snow storm, so it would take about two hours to get there, that was the longest two hours of our lives. Every little noise or creak we thought it was somebody coming for us, and we had no curtains, so didn't know if we were been watched from outside or not.

When she did get to us, she told us about a white van that had been driving on the wrong side of the road going out of the town with its lights off. It sounded very weird to me as nobody drives in a snow storm with lights off unless they don't want to be seen. She had kindly put us up in a room in the apt/hotel and we were so exhausted at this stage, we couldn't even think straight we knew we had to get home, as we had no money, and nobody that would be able to protect us here But Alaska has one main road in and on main road out that is it and we had no car, there was no transport in the form of trains to the lower 49 states and the flights were all very expensive.

As much as we loved Alaska and hated having to consider leaving we now didn't have a choice, we had no home, no money, nobody to help us and god knows who was after us . We slept like babies that night it was one of the first nights in a few that we hadn't been in fear, yet we could see no light at the end of the tunnel. We then started to panic that because we had left without telling anybody that perhaps people will think that we had something to do with those fires we didn't, but we couldn't take the chance of our house been next whether it was a coincidence or whether it was one of the scum after us. There was no way we could just sit back and wait for their next move no we had to make the move and leave and leave fast and that is exactly what we did . In looking back it was most certainly the right decision to make at the time.

We headed to Anchorage, we stopped in Wasilla for a night then down to the Airport in Anchorage there was no point in staying longer in Wasilla even though we had a place to stay and were warm at the end of the day we had to leave and as fast and as inexpensive as possible. Now one of the luxuries in Alaska is that it is so inaccessible however in our circumstances, we really needed the opposite. When we got to the airport, we had no flights booked, no were to stay, and very little money. I had run out of ideas at this stage, so I spoke to a police officer and told him our story he was able to verify what id told him with our contacts in Vegas so they knew we were genuine. Yet none of the airlines would even help us to get to the lower 49 states . As at least that way we would have more options, no we were stuck and were total sitting ducks again. The officer told me that he was making a call to somebody who might help us and I spoke to them on the phone , I explained our scenario and that we basically needed help, she spoke to the officer and they told us that we were been brought somewhere safe that would help us to get out of Alaska. Well the people we met, the place we stayed all was so overwhelming. Here were strangers willing to help us yet in our own country, we couldn't even get an order of protection it just seemed like two worlds. We spoke with them in-debt and obviously for their confidentiality reasons I can't go into detail but after a week there, were we were safe. We had managed to organize flights home. We offered to totally reimburse the fares and any funds for our stay there,

However the agency said that they had funds and that if we wanted to head home that they would pay the entire bill. Not only did they do that they gave us a visa prepaid card with USD100 on it for the flights as you can only use credit cards for food or drink on the aircraft. They had us in full protection we were brought to the gate with police escort and we were heading home. I cried for the entire 21 hour journey as Alaska was where we wanted to be and only for we would have had to stay there as illegals until our visas were sorted ,and I was too nervous to do that, I would have stayed we all would have .We are working at present to go back to the USA and to live our lives there.

We want to give back to the country and the many people that helped us, as strangers who have now become our friends and family in this wonderful state and country. The weird thing is that Alaska is known like Ireland as The Emerald Isle. The trip was horrendous it wore us all down, and took so much out of us, as we had so many flights and so much on our minds. Yet we knew when we got back to Ireland once again all protection was gone and we were once again on our own. The Chef and Tony been Irish can come and go as they please and they still have plenty of influential contacts here so it would be easy to find us, as for Bas he has always found us and either Bas or The Chef / Tony want rid of me so whichever one does it first than clearly benefits the other. MS 13 I have no idea about as we did no wrong on them, all those workers and suppliers and this man Meco should to be paid the money they worked for, but again it is amazing what knowing the right people can do for you especially in Ireland and the United States. My kids and I are to this scum chef and his partners in crime mere statistics, we are a thorn in his side. But I am a thorn that won't go away, until the day that he is held accountable for his crimes against everybody. He may have won a few of the battles but the war isn't over yet and justice will prevail at the end of the day. I intend with Jake to have ringside seats for the day that they are held accountable in court in the United States of America.

As for Rory, well as I said earlier he had turned into his dad however as bad as that was, and as bad and saddened as it is to watch an amazing talent be ruined by wanting to be somebody you are not, the worst thing in my eyes is that he did exactly as he was told by the chef and Tony .And the brainless Rory went and married a girl who is an American Muslim he is not .We saw this on Facebook. But as an abuser then he is in heaven as he can do as he pleases under Sharia Law to his now wife. This marriage was very much against some of her families wishes and within a few months of them been together he married her and I believe that she is either pregnant with his child or has had a baby for him. I did try to warn her of his abuse, his affairs but she would not listen so I guess she will have to find out the hard way in life .My heart does go out to her though.

Bas he got the phone call about the wedding, as he and Rory now good friends ,but sure they are no different to each other. I had never met this unfortunate girl, I had only spoken to her on the phone. I tried to warn her tried to tell her that he was using her for a visa, that he had sexual encounters with at least 4 other women that I knew of when he was in Vegas and she was in New York but he did as Bas did with me, he got out of the mess with his lies and she told me I was a witch and from that day on I have neither spoken to or seen my son. The last time I saw him, he was driving off with the Chef to the airport in Vegas both heading back to New York that was in August 2012. He had all the signs of an abuser growing up, he also lived with one and now he has in my eyes become one and has full control of this woman which is very sad. It saddens me greatly that one man who had at one stage in his life a talent for cooking and was famous for same let the financial gain of that life in the high society change him so much, that he actually does believe his own lies. That he has now and will always until stopped scam the innocent people who work for him ,brainwash the young chefs that train under him, not pay suppliers, build up huge debts, ensuring lots of small businesses go broke and the one thing that he will do is laugh all the way to the bank.

I still have all the evidence it is in a bank safe fault in the USA so he will never get it. And it is available to any and all agencies within the USA who would love to shut him down and to stop his crimes against innocent people .They can't say that they don't know him they do but as of yet he isn't red flagged on the warning systems in place, this is one chef who really needs to get out of the kitchen and fast. He did incidentally during the writing of this book go on to commit the exact same scams and frauds in Vegas, in the exact premises that I said he would, and yet he has so far gotten away with it again. I believe that he has now left Vegas and has now set up in Beverly Hills California and has a new restaurant up and running until he is caught out there too. His sole reason for opening these restaurants is for financial gain, and to avoid accountability, he moves states and as Tony is the silent partner he just washes his money through the restaurants.

CHAPTER 12

SIGNS OF AN ABUSIVE PERSONALITY

Most people think that they wouldn't be stupid enough to fall victim to an abuser, but nobody plans it and for sure nobody wants it .But these people who abuse others are extremely clever they have a game plan and there are certain traits that all abusers have in common. Not all of the traits will initially be present but I guarantee you that by the time you decide to get out of this abusive relationship you will realize that this entire chapter is probably reading like a diary of your life. But remember just because it reads like your life, doesn't mean that you can't take your control and your right to your own life back hence stopping the cycle. You need to do this before your own children are learning that abuse is normal and then when they grow up, they will either live the life you did in an abusive relationship or they will be the abuser and neither of these types of scenarios are what any parent wants for any of their children.

Here is an extensive list of signs to look for in a potential abuser not all people with these traits will turn into those that abuse others but in general a lot of them do .

JEALOUSY

At the start of a relationship he or she will try to tell you that their jealousy is only because they love you so much. They will accuse you of flirting with other men /women and will get annoyed at any time that you spend away from them with other people including your own family.

CONTROLLING BEHAVIOUR

Again at the start they will make out that they are only trying to help you in making decisions or for your safety. But in time the abuser will escalate to a position where it makes your life very hard to escape from. He / She will eventually assume full control of all finances within the relationship hence ensuring that they can control where and when you go out and what you do.

QUICK INVOLVEMENT

A lot of times an abused man or woman has only been involved with their abuser initially for a short period of time, before they moved in together, got engaged then got married. They make you feel that you are in the wrong by wanting to take things slowly, but they are the ones in the wrong, as they are pressuring you to commit to the relationship a lot quicker than you want .But in order not to lose them you do what they ask.

UNREALISTIC EXPECTATIONS

An abuser will expect you to take care of their every whim, simply everything that they want or need in life you will be expected to provide for them .This includes emotional, domestic, physically and sexually you are their slave.

ISOLATION

This is one of the main signs and in almost all cases there will be some form of isolation .As once they isolate you from your family your friends ,the outside world as you know it then they have control. They can stop you using the phone, the car, working, financially and they will accuse those people in your life that love you and who want to help you as been trouble makers and trying to get you away from him or her.

BLAMES OTHERS FOR PROBLEMS

No matter what happens in life it is not their fault. An abuser will always blame anybody and everybody else for any obstacle that has gotten in their way of their aims in life. As the victim you will be blamed for every single thing that is wrong in your abusers life, irrespective of the reason for the situation that they are in .Your abuser has one aim and one aim only to blame you for everything and in some way in their minds that justifies their behavior and abuse of you.

BLAMES OTHERS FOR FEELINGS

An abuser is very manipulative and they will use this against you they will try to make you feel guilty if you don't do as they want. For example they might say well your hurting me or you don t love me by not doing what I want, this isn't the case it Is just part of their overall game plan.

HYPERSENSITIVITY

Most abusers are extremely easy to insult and no matter how small or insignificant the matter been spoken about is, they will take it as an attack on them personally. They will see this as the highest of insults on them personally even if it was not intended as an insult or if wasn't even been directed at them, they will seize the moment and use it to their own advantage.

CONTROL & ENTITLEMENT ABUSE

This is another form of Domestic Violence and is very prevalent yet not widely spoken about. This is where the abuser has full control over money, property, who you talk to, what you wear, where you go, when you have sex and how you raise your children. The feeling of entitlement means that you feel you are the owner of something. An abuser will think that he/she owns you and therefor can tell you what to do when they feel like it. Remember that it is not in any way your fault that you are the victim of abuse, you did not ask for it and you sure as hell don't deserve it

BARRIERS TO LEAVING FOR VICTIM'S
OF
DOMESTIC VIOLENCE

SURVIVAL

You have very real fears that he or she will follow you wherever you end up and will kill you. Very often these are just not fears, they are based on real threats to the victim by the abuser. Through the abuse that they have suffered with them over a period of time or years, they know more than anybody that it is a very real possiblility that if he/she finds you that you will be killed or injured.

ECONOMIC DEPENDENCE

How will you survive without their help financially? How will you feed the kids? How will you put a roof over their head ? These are the fears that have arisen from his/her control of your family finances.

PARENTING

Most people say that children need to have both their parents in their lives, and some see it that it is better to have an abusive parent in their life than to just have the one. This is wrong one good parent is a million times better for the child than living in an abusive environment.

RELIGOUS – FAMILY BELIEVES

A family should stay together in the eyes of some religions and in some families at any cost. But it is not fair that children should suffer, solely because others think that they don't deserve to have a better `life. Family is great but it can also in this situation be very wrong for all involved.

FEAR OF BEEN ALONE – SECURITY

The victim feels that he or she cannot manage without the partner their abuser in their lives. They feel that it would be too much for them with the kids, schools, work, utilities, and life in general so they stick it out for all the wrong reasons.

LOYALTY

Sometimes this is partly based on religious believes ,but if your with your partner even if they are abusing you. Sadly some feel that you should have some form of loyalty to them. That you don't just leave him or her, as they are abusing you or your family. You try to convince yourself that they are simply sick or ill.

PITY

You feel sorry in some way for your abuser you try to justify all that has happened into some rational reasoning. Even though you can't ever do this, you still have that feeling for them that you just cannot leave.

NOT A TYPICAL VICTIM

A lot of reports of Domestic Violence are not made solely out of embarrassment or over stigmas that ignorant people have in the world. It is very hard for men, gays, lesbians and the elderly to report any form of abuse. As they feel that they will either be judged or ignored due to their personal situations and that is extremely sad. Men are just as much victims as women are they just don't   report it through the taboo and embarrassment .

WANTING TO HELP

At this stage you are so under their control that you think that if you stay that perhaps in some way you can help them get better. This behavior is not like a cold or flu, you can't make it better with some medication it is a long road for recovery for both the victim and the abusers.

SUICIDE THREATS

Once again the abuser will use their manipulation, of your mind to make you believe that he or she will actually kill themselves and commit suicide if you ever leave them. This is just a threat as they are playing any card that they can think of in order to keep you as their victim. As the day you leave and walk out that door you are no longer a victim, no longer a statistic, you are a SURVIVOR.

DENIAL

You tell yourself that it is not that bad that there are a lot of people out there that are in worse situations than you, and perhaps there are. But you are not leading their life and they are not leading yours. Worry about your own life and safety and then when you get that under control then try and help the others. But stop denying your own situations severity.

LOVE

You convince yourself that it is the violence that you want to stop not the relationship ,but this cannot happen as they are both intertwined with each other. Yes on his or her good days you might see the person that you fell in love with but these days will be few and far between, you must not let these feeling overshadow the abuse and violence that is more prevalent than the love .The first day that he or she made you their victim was the last day that they had the right to your love.

DUTY / OBLIGATION

You took an oath when you married your partner and said till death do us part ,but you don't want this to happen. As when you are abused it's your life that is at risk at his or her hand. You must remember that you neither owe nor are obligated to them in anyway.

GUILT

The skill used by an abuser over their victim in my eyes is total brain washing. They make you the victim actually believe that you are to blame for their drinking, their violence, their affairs. But that is what they want, that is the key to their control over you and the key to their abuse continuing or stopping.

RESPONSIBILITY

Women in general are conditioned to be the ones in families to fix the problem or that the responsibility for the emotional upheaval is theirs to solve. Well it is not, their only responsibility is to keep themselves safe and their children. If they have any and get out of the relationship as fast as possible.

SHAME & HUMILIATION

It is embarrassing and very humiliating to let those around you know the truth about your life. As for so many years you lived a life of lies two lives on one hand you had the image you portrayed to the outside world and then the actual life that you lived behind closed doors .The shame is all your abusers to carry not yours in anyway.

IDENTITY

Women in general have been socialized to think that they need a partner in life whether that be an abusive one or not at least there not alone. A partner that is abusive is not worth having .

UNFOUNDED OPTIMISM

If I believe in him enough then perhaps he will change and things will get better, despite the evidence to the contrary. He/she won't change as this is their way of life now and they enjoy having the control and power and nothing and nobody will be allowed to take that from them.

INTERNALIZATION OF ABUSERS WORDS

This is one of the most horrifying thoughts that any victim has ,it is one where you actually do believe that you deserve this treatment, that you do deserve his/her punches, his/her verbal insults. Nobody in this world, not even the abuser themselves deserve to be treated with this lack of respect. They have simply brainwashed you into thinking that you have done wrong in life and that this is your punishment.

ALCOHOL IS THE CAUSE

Anybody who has ever lived in any type of abusive situation will know once they leave that life behind them, that all that was said to them by their abuser in order to ease his or her own guilt was lies. Many people will blame alcohol for the violence and this is a myth. There is certainly a connection between alcohol and domestic violence but IT is not the reason for the abuse. Abusers use the violence for one reason and one reason only and that's because they can. In a lot of cases most certainly, some will get a lot more aggressive when they even have a minute amount of alcohol in their system, but remember millions of people around the world drink alcohol and they are not all abusers, and they don't all commit a crime. Abusers simply want to try and justify their actions any way possible.

RAPES ARE CAUSED ONLY BY STRANGERS

Statistics show that most rapes or sexual assaults are carried out by somebody that you would know and who until now would have trusted. A lot of assaults are either carried out in your own home or in the home of the abuser. Rape is not your fault you never asked for it and NO means NO .Even if you didn't fight back during the assault don't blame yourself, as by not fighting back you stayed alive to tell your story .If you make any effort to decline his or her sexual contact then that is Rape irrespective of whether you fought back or not.

DOMESTIC VIOLENCE IS ONLY AGAINST WOMEN

WRONG this is probably one of the worst things that anybody can go through in their lives. However as a man, not only does it destroy you as a person, it also strips you of all your male characteristics. Where you are the stronger one, you are the one to fight and to protect yet you cannot protect yourself .Men are victims of violence and abuse and rape all around the world and because of the stigma and in my opinion peoples ignorance, they hide their abuse and assaults. It is easier to hide them then to have the humiliation of telling and trying to explain as to why you didn't stop it. If this stigma was lifted and everybody actually learned more about the fact that a large amount of men are raped as well as abused ,then perhaps these victims can stop been victims and like women in the world get the help and support that they not only need but what they deserve.

CHAPTER 13

ARE YOU A VICTIM? – ESCAPE NOW

Below is some information that will help you to decide if you are concerned whether or not you are a victim of abuse. It shows you additional signs to look out for, that perhaps you wouldn't normally think are symptoms of a potential abuser. If your partner even has just one of the signs then he/she is an abuser. He/she may not as of yet be at the peak of their abuse, but once he/she starts and sees the control that they have this will ignite their desire to totally control you in all aspects of your life.

If you are lucky you will escape before the abuse and violence Escalates .Use the details in this chapter to gather together the main items that you will need to initially get away from him or her. But at all times to stay alive and to be safe is paramount ,if you can't get all ready to escape just bide your time and know that once you go that there is no going back .And that you have done the right thing, even if you are scared senseless in time you will realize how right you were.

Some warning signs that are definitely signals for a potential abuser are the following, these are what I call the hidden signs that a lot of people may not realize .But the person who is showing them is starting on his or her path to been an abuser in one way or another.

CRUELTY TO ANIMALS OR CHILDREN – this sadly is one of the main warning signs .They have no hesitation in hurting or killing any animal for their own personal enjoyment and would slap or scare with verbal abuse perhaps a young child or baby for wetting the bed or for getting sick .

VERBALLY -this type of abuse is in my experience one of the worst. As he or she will say what they know will hurt you, but also be extremely cruel, degrading, call you names and insult you P in front of your children. At some stage in front of others. They take away your self- confidence by putting down any of your accomplishments in life, solely because they can.

PERSONALITY - as they say you never know what goes on
behind closed doors and it is so true. Outside the house they will be
the picture perfect partner and in general it is men who are the
abuser, although in some circumstances it is the reverse. But he will be so
polite, charming, helpful to others that he ensures that with this behavior,
he is seen as a saint. Therefor controlling the fact that others haven't seen
the real him and hence keeping you quiet, as you think nobody would
believe you, but they would.

THREATS OF VIOLENCE - this includes any type of physical force to
control their partner, most people don t threaten their partner as they have
respect for them .But abusers don't think their victim is entitled to respect
hence them been threatening to you, and in convincing you that if anybody
else was with you that they would do the same, That's rubbish its them
trying to justify their actions to themselves.

BREAKING OBJECTS – a lot of times they will break an item that is
either valuable or sentimental to you as they know the hurt and upset that
it will cause. Some abusers will also threaten to break something if you
don't do as they ask.

ANY FORCE DURING AN ARGUMENT – This can include your
abuser holding down his /her partner physically restrain you from
leaving the house or room, pushing ,shoving, hitting ,kicking you and
telling you that you will listen to them whether you like it or not one way
or the other .These actions are all abusive.

PLAYFUL USE OF FORCE IN SEX -This area includes a lot
however some of the main features are restraining of their partner
against their wishes during sex .Acting out any fantasy in which
the victim is helpless .Initiating sex when you don't want it or when
your tired or asleep or even sick. The abuser doesn't care about the needs
or wishes of the victim he/she will have a child like tantrum to get what
they want including sulking, aggression and manipulation in order to get
their own way.

RIGID SEX ROLES – In general the victim is usually a woman, her
abuser will see her as his own personal slave to serve him anyway he
wants and when he wants. He will consider her inferior to him, ensure that

she is degraded by having to do menial tasks is stupid and is unable to be a whole person without a relationship. What the
abuser forgets is that he doesn't have a relationship, he has a victim that he controls but this is not in his way of thinking. Once you start to feel that you want to leave and that you know you deserve a better life, unless you are one of the very lucky ones who has no financial worries and somewhere to go to, you are going to have to make sure that you plan this escape .As that basically is what you leaving is an escape from hell.

Especially if you have any children you have be extremely careful that the abuser doesn't find out about your plans .If your children are not old enough to understand not to say anything then don't tell them ,make and prepare all when they are not around and in particular when and only when you are sure that your abuser is not around. Otherwise it is putting your safety at risk as they never want to lose you, as that would mean they have lost control, In some situations they would feel it is better to kill you then to have you walk away so be extra cautious and play clever .

Prepare a bag with what you know you will need for your escape but try to include the following items.

1.Cash if you have any way of getting money and to hiding it from the abuser try and get as much as is safely possible.

2.A current Family Photo of you and your children also one of your abuser, as it can be put on file with police. And at a safe house so staff will know what he looks like, hence ensuring your safety at the facility.

3. Warm clothing for you and the children, it is a lot better to wear lots of light layers of clothes as these are warmer than bulky items. So plenty of vests and undergarments as well as tights for under what your wearing.

4. Identity documents for you and your children, if they have their own passports make sure that they are valid and well hidden. You will need them to travel anywhere, even if it is internally within your own country. If they have visas take them to .Also ensure you have their social security numbers and birth certificates and don't forget to include your own.

5. Medication this is extremely vital as if you or the kids are on any

type of prescribed medication you will need to ensure that you have
at least enough of an emergency supply with you. As once you leave your
mindset is going to be more on staying safe, rather than finding
prescriptions and medication.

6. Prepaid Credit Cards try to get at least one of these and put any
money that you can on it before you leave. That way there is no
paper trail and you have use of a credit card if you need to reserve
any train, bus or air tickets. Since he/she probably had control of all the
finances he/she will also have his accounts set up online, so if you use
your ATM card he would have a paper trail .No paper trail as if you don't
have one he/she cannot find you. If you have a check book take this solely
as an emergency and only use in that case and preferably as a guarantee
that isn't cashed.

7. Small valuable items like jewelry .these you can use as for a dual reason
as they are also items that you can sell easily with your id in any pawn
shop .So if you are stuck for money then at least you will have a way to
get some .As without money you may feel you have to go back to your
abuser and that is what he or she is counting on.

8. Prepaid Mobile / Cell phone try if at all possible again to have at
least two phones with you even if one of them is that of your kids it's a
back- up. Again if prepaid then it cannot be tracked, as it is not a
registered phone, no paper trail.

9. Entertainment I know this sounds crazy but you need to ensure
that you have things with you that the kids can be kept busy with, If
they have a game boy or something similar or books, games, not
heavy items to carry but ones that they will be able to relax and have a
sense of normality with. But remember No Internet Activity

10. Documentation if you have any protection or safety orders
make sure that you keep them with you. If at all possible try and have the
original order or legal documents kept either by somebody who you can
trust or in a bank safe ,just keep the copies of same with you, that way you
have them to show the relevant authorities.

Your abuser will not be able to destroy them if he or she gets hold of the original, try to get into their mindset and stay one step ahead of them. If you are renting a house or have a mortgage with your abuser, than take copies of the payments with you.

11. Snacks and food that the kids and you will eat that doesn't need to be heated or cooked. It is easy now of days to get nutritional food that they will all eat that is not too expensive but is easy enough to fill the hunger pangs when leaving.

12. An extra set of car keys and if at all possible two copies of any Utility bills that have your name on them. As if you need to rent anywhere, you will need them also for opening any new bank account in your own name.

13 Important phone numbers to include but just as a guide your solicitor /attorney, your medical provider, your own immediate family ,medical insurers ,local shelter, police. Remember that by leaving your abuser you are not taking the children away from their mom or dad .You are taking them out of a very dangerous ,volatile and horrible lifestyle in order not just to save your elf but to save them to. As learned behavior can and does happen ,and you don't want your children to turn into your abuser in the future.

The kids might not realize that you are doing the right thing by leaving, but in time when they see that they don't have to see or hear abuse or violence they will realize that you were right and they will never ever want to live that abusive life again. By planning to leave you are making the first big step, you have realized and decided that you deserve better, that you need to live your life not simply exist in it. So once that thought of escape comes into your head just focus on that focus on the end result of you with a life with your children if you have any and your life back in your control without fear or abuse.

Now just because you leave, doesn't mean that a magic wand is been waved and all the pain and suffering will vanish. That is another step and a lot of hard work, but do it one step at a time and each time you reach to the top of that step, then you are only one step further away from your goal .If it is possible to get your items together, to leave in a bag and if you have a friend or family member that you can trust, maybe ask them if they could hold it for you. That way when you leave if you happen to get times wrong and he/she is there it will look like you are just going out for a walk or to collect kids or shops you can think of an excuse.

But if he/she sees that bag, then he will erupt and that could be extremely dangerous for you all. Take control from that first thought of escape you have to believe that you can do it and you will. Look at what you have survived through up to this day, and this day is the first day of the rest of our life, in Your control, so enjoy it and be free.

Make contact with not only the police in your local area, but ask them to help you with advising the police and schools in the area that you need to move to .Get as much in writing as you can from the police and apply for every protection and safety order that is available to you. Contact a shelter in the area that you intend to move to, this will not be for a permanent basis it is just to help you get back on your feet, consider it a stepping stone to your new life.

But there protection and help is invaluable In certain states within the USA your child can be enrolled in schools without a paper trail, there are particular programs for this but you need to let the school authorities aware of the situation.

In the United States not even the police can enter a shelter for abused women or children as they are there for protection. The shelter can help to organize not only safe housing for you, relocation to another area, financial help and aid and applications for same,. Schooling if required if you have children and admissions to hospitals, and all other services without there been any paper trail. Although nobody wants to go to a shelter, and have to live there even temporarily, until their situation is been rectified it is a lot better than living with your abuser and his/her abuse, at least here you are all safe.

In the next chapter of the book is a very detailed list of organizations and shelters all around the world. There is at least one in every country so although it may not be in your area if you need help all that you have to do is to call them and they will tell you who to contact and where to go in your immediate vicinity. In certain countries especially the United States the laws for victims and families of Domestic Violence are fantastic. They can even organize for you to be collected from where you are and brought to their shelter by the police.

In certain states and in particular in Alaska there is a 60 sec response time from the police to the shelter and there is always some form of police patrols in the immediate area. It is hard to ask, and it is also hard to say what has been going on, but you are entitled to be safe and that is what all of these organizations will do for you. The more you hide the more control you give your abuser, take away that control and you see them for the small sad people that they are. They are bullies and bullies always prefer to be the boss of you in every aspect of your life.

Once you are safe and you know that he/she cannot get to you, then you can start to contact your old trusted friends and family, tell them what was going on don't hide it, you will be amazed at the help and support that they will give you .In a lot of cases they probably knew themselves that the abuse was happening, but they didn't know what to say or to do in order to help you.

But now you have come to them, they will help and that itself will give you the confidence to stay away from your abuser and to if possible get justice for your abuse .However this isn't always possible due to lack of physical evidence and non-reporting of crimes within the statutes of Limitations. But the best result that you can have is to wake up every morning and know that you are now free, and your abuser, well they are now alone and the ones who simply now exist were as you are the one to live.

CHAPTER 14

WORLDWIDE CONTACTS

In Europe and America you can contact your local police and they will help put you in touch with the relevant agencies that can help you,If you don't have your local police number than contact the emergency services number for your country .

In general 911 can be used in Europe and America just insure that you have the details in your head .Sometimes it is better to ring the emergency services as you will get immediate response and cane ensure that your safe as their response time would be faster than that of the shelters due to the demand for their services .

AMERICA

ALASKA
AWAIC SHELTER-ANCHORAGE
100w 13th Avenue
Anchorage,
Alaska 99501
24hr Crisis Line-- 907 272 0100
Direct Number --- 907 279 9581
website> www.awaic.org

ALABAMA- **Coalition Against Domestic Violence**
P. O. Box 4762
Montgomery, AL 36101
(334) 832-4842 Fax: (334) 832-4803
(800) 650-6522 Hotline
Website: www.acadv.org
Email: acadv@acadv.org

ALASKA - **Network on Domestic and Sexual Violence**
130 Seward Street, Room 209
Juneau, AK 99801
(907) 586-3650 Fax: (907) 463-4493
Website: www.andvsa.org

ARIZONA Coalition Against Domestic Violence
2800 N. Central Ave., Suite 1570
Phoenix, AZ 85004
(602) 279-2900 Fax: (602) 279-2980
(800) 782-6400 Nationwide
Website: www.azcadv.org
Email: acadv@azadv.org

ARKANSAS **Coalition Against Domestic Violence**
1401 W. Capitol Avenue, Suite 170
Little Rock, AR 72201
(501) 907-5612 Fax: (501) 907-5618
(800) 269-4668 Nationwide
Website: www.domesticpeace.com
Email: kbangert@domesticpeace.com

CALIFORNIA **Partnership to End Domestic Violence**
P. O. Box 1798
Sacramento, CA 95812
(916) 444-7163 Fax: (916) 444-7165
(800) 524-4765 Nationwide
Website: www.cpedv.org
Email: info@cpedv.org

COLORADO **Coalition Against Domestic Violence**
P. O. Box 18902
Denver, CO 80218
(303) 831-9632 Fax: (303) 832-7067
(888) 788-7091
Website: www.ccadv.org

CONNECTICUT **Coalition Against Domestic Violence**
90 Pitkin Street
East Hartford, CT 06108
(860) 282-7899 Fax: (860) 282-7892
(800) 281-1481 In State
(888) 774-2900 In State DV Hotline
Website: www.ctcadv.org
Email: info@ctcadv.org

DELAWARE **Coalition Against Domestic Violence**
100 W. 10th Street, #703
Wilmington, DE 19801
(302) 658-2958 Fax: (302) 658-5049
(800) 701-0456 Statewide
Website: www.dcadv.org
Email: dcadv@dcadv.org

DC **Coalition Against Domestic Violence**
1718 P Street, Suite T-6
Washington, DC 20036
(202) 299-1181 Fax: (202) 299-1193
Website: www.dccadv.org
Email: help@dccadv.org

FLORIDA **Coalition Against Domestic Violence**
425 Office Plaza
Tallahassee, FL 32301
(850) 425-2749 Fax: (850) 425-3091
(850) 621-4202 TDD
(800) 500-1119 In State
Website: www.fcadv.org

GEORGIA **Coalition Against Domestic Violence**
P.O. Box 7532, Athens, GA 30604
Atlanta, GA 30354
(404) 209-0280 Fax: (404) 766-3800
Website: www.gcadv.org

GUAM **Coalition Against Sexual Assault and FV**
P.O. Box 1093
Hagatna, GU 96932
(671) 479-2277

HAWAII **State Coalition Against Domestic Violence**
716 Umi Street, Suite 210
Honolulu, HI 96819-2337
(808) 832-9316 Fax: (808) 841-6028
Website: www.hscadv.org

IDAHO **Coalition Against Sexual & Domestic Violence**
815 Park Boulevard, #140
Boise, ID 83712
(208) 384-0419 Fax: (208) 331-0687
(888) 293-6118 Nationwide
Website: www.idvsa.org
Email: domvio@mindspring.com

ILLINOIS **Coalition Against Domestic Violence**
801 S. 11th Street
Springfield, IL 62703
(217) 789-2830 Fax: (217) 789-1939
Website: www.ilcadv.org
Email: ilcadv@ilcadv.org

INDIANA **Coalition Against Domestic Violence**
1915 W. 18th Street
Indianapolis, IN 46202
(317) 917-3685 Fax: (317) 917-3695
(800) 332-7385 In State
Website: www.violenceresource.org
Email: icadv@violenceresource.org

IOWA **Coalition against Domestic Violence**
515 28th Street, #104
Des Moines, IA 50312
178
Survivors Not Statistics
(515) 244-8028 Fax: (515) 244-7417
(800) 942-0333 In State Hotline
Website: www.icadv.org

KANSAS **Coalition against Sexual and Domestic Violence**
634 SW Harrison Street
Topeka, KS 66603
(785) 232-9784 Fax: (785) 266-1874
Website: www.kcsdv.org
Email: coalition@kcsdv.org

KENTUCKY **Domestic Violence Association**
P.O. Box 356
Frankfort, KY 40602
(502) 209-5381 Fax: (502) 695-2488
Website: www.kdva.org

LOUISANA **Coalition Against Domestic Violence**
P.O. Box 77308
Baton Rouge, LA 70879
(225) 752-1296 Fax: (225) 751-8927
Website: www.lcadv.org

MAINE **Coalition to End Domestic Violence**
170 Park Street
Bangor, ME 04401
(207) 941-1194 Fax: (207) 941-2327
Website: www.mcedv.org
Email: info@mcedv.org

MARYLAND Network Against Domestic Violence
6911 Laurel-Bowie Road, #309
Bowie, MD 20715
(301) 352-4574 Fax: (301) 809-0422
(800) 634-3577 Nationwide
Website: www.mnadv.org
Email: mnadv@aol.com

MASSACHUSETTS - Jane Doe, Inc Coalition Against Sexual Assault and
Domestic Violence
14 Beacon Street, #507
Boston, MA 02108
(617) 248-0922 Fax: (617) 248-0902
TTY/TTD: (617) 263-2200
Website: www.janedoe.org
Email: info@janedoe.org

MICHIGAN **Coalition against Domestic & Sexual Violence**
3893 Okemos Road, #B-2
Okemos, MI 48864
(517) 347-7000 Fax: (517) 347-1377
TTY: (517) 381-8470
Website: www.mcadsv.org
Email: general@mcadsv.org

MINNESOTA **Coalition for Battered Women**
1821 University Avenue West, #S-112
St. Paul, MN 55104
(651) 646-6177 Fax: (651) 646-1527
Crisis Line: (651) 646-0994
(800) 289-6177 Nationwide
Website: www.mcbw.org
Email: mcbw@mcbw.org

MISSISSIPI **Coalition Against Domestic Violence**
P.O. Box 4703
Jackson, MS 39296
(601) 981-9196 Fax: (601) 981-2501
Website: www.mcadv.org

MISSOURI **Coalition Against Domestic Violence**
718 East Capitol Avenue
Jefferson City, MO 65101
(573) 634-4161 Fax: (573) 636-3728
Website: www.mocadv.org
Email: mcadv@sockets.net

MONTANA **Coalition Against Domestic & Sexual Violence**
P.O. Box 818
Helena, MT 59624
(406) 443-7794 Fax: (406) 443-7818
(888) 404-7794 Nationwide
Website: www.mcadsv.com
Email: mcadsv@mt.net

NEBRASKA **Domestic Violence and Sexual Assault Coalition**
1000 O Street, #102
Lincoln, NE 68508
(402) 476-6256 Fax: (402) 476-6806
(877) 215-0167 Spanish In State
Website: www.ndvsac.org
Email: info@ndvsac.org

NEVADA **Network Against Domestic Violence**
220 S. Rock Blvd. Suite 7,
Reno, NV 89502-2355
(775) 828-1115 Fax: (775) 828-9911
(800) 500-1556 In State
Website: www.nnadv.org

NEW HAMPSHIRE Coalition Against Domestic and Sexual Violence
P.O. Box 353
Concord, NH 03302
(603) 224-8893 Fax: (603) 228-6096
(866) 644-3574 In State
Website: www.nhcadsv.org

NEW JERSEY **Coalition for Battered Women**
1670 Whitehorse Hamilton Square
Trenton, NJ 08690
(609) 584-8107 Fax: (609) 584-9750
(800) 572-7233 In State
Website: www.njcbw.org
Email: info@njcbw.org

NEW MEXICO **State Coalition Against Domestic Violence**
200 Oak NE, #4
Albuquerque, NM 87106
(505) 246-9240 Fax: (505) 246-9434
(800) 773-3645 In State
Website: www.nmcadv.org

NEW YORK STATE **Coalition Against Domestic Violence**
350 New Scotland Avenue
Albany, NY 12054
(518) 482-5464 Fax: (518) 482-3807
(800) 942-6906 English-In State
(800) 942-6908 Spanish-In State

Website: www.nyscadv.org
Email: nyscadv@nyscadv.org

NORTH CAROLINA **Coalition Against Domestic Violence**
115 Market Street, #400
Durham, NC 27701
(919) 956-9124 Fax: (919) 682-1449
(888) 232-9124 Nation wide
Website: www.nccadv.org

NORTH DAKOTA **Council on Abused Women's Services**
418 E. Rosser Avenue, #320
Bismark, ND 58501
(701) 255-6240 Fax: (701) 255-1904
(888) 255-6240 Nationwide
Website: www.ndcaws.org
Email: ndcaws@ndcaws.org

OHIO. DOMESTIC VIOLENCE NETWORK
4807 Evanswood Drive, Suite 201
COLUMBUS, OHIO 43229
614-781-9651 (phone)
614-781-9652 (fax)
800-934-9840 (national)
Website: www.odvn.org
Email: info@odvn.org

OKLAHOMA **Coalition Against Domestic Violence and Sexual Assault**
3815 N. Santa Fe Ave., Suite 124
Oklahoma City, OK 73118
(405) 524-0700 Fax: (405) 524-0711
Website: www.ocadvsa.org

OREGON **Coalition Against Domestic and Sexual Violence**
380 SE Spokane Street, #100
Portland, OR 97202
(503) 230-1951 Fax: (503) 230-1973
Website: www.ocadsv.com

PENNSYLVANNIA **Coalition Against Domestic Violence**
6400 Flank Drive, #1300
Harrisburg, PA 17112
(717) 545-6400 Fax: (717) 545-9456
(800) 932-4632 Nationwide
Website: www.pcadv.org

PUERTO RICO
The Office of Women Advocates
Box 11382
Fernandez Juancus Station
Santurce, PR 00910
(787) 721-7676 Fax: (787) 725-9248

RHODE ISLAND **Coalition Against Domestic Violence**
422 Post Road, #202
Warwick, RI 02888
(401) 467-9940 Fax: (401) 467-9943
(800) 494-8100 In State
Website: www.ricadv.org
Email: ricadv@ricadv.org

SOUTH CAROLINA **Coalition Against Domestic Violence and Sexual Assault**
P.O. Box 7776
Columbia, SC 29202
(803) 256-2900 Fax: (803) 256-1030
(800) 260-9293 Nationwide
Website: www.sccadvasa.org

SOUTH DAKOTA **Coalition Against Domestic Violence & Sexual Assault**
P.O. Box 141
Pierre, SD 57501
(605) 945-0869 Fax: (605) 945-0870
(800) 572-9196 Nationwide
Website: www.southdakotacoalition.org
Email: sdcadvsa@rapidnet.com

TENNESSEE **Coalition Against Domestic and Sexual Violence**
P.O. Box 120972
Nashville, TN 37212
(615) 386-9406 Fax: (615) 383-2967
(800) 289-9018 In State
Website: www.tcadsv.org
Email **tcadsv@tcadsv.org**

TEXAS Council on Family Violence
P.O. Box 161810
Austin, TX 78716
(512) 794-1133 Fax: (512) 794-1199
(800) 525-1978 In State

Website: www.tcfv.org

ST CROIX **Women's Coalition of St. Croix**
Box 2734
Christiansted
St. Croix, VI 00822
(340) 773-9272 Fax: (340) 773-9062
Website: www.wcstx.com
Email: wcscstx@attglobal.net

UTAH **Domestic Violence Council**
205 North 400 West,
Salt Lake City, 84103
(801) 521-5544 Fax: (801) 521-5548
Website: www.udvac.org

VERMONT **Network Against Domestic Violence and Sexual Assault**
P.O. Box 405
Montpelier, VT 05601
(802) 223-1302 Fax: (802) 223-6943
Website: www.vtnetwork.org
Email: vtnetwork@vtnetwork.org

VIRGINIANS **Against Domestic Violence**
2850 Sandy Bay Road, #101
Williamsburg, VA 23185
(757) 221-0990 Fax: (757) 229-1553
(800) 838-8238 Nationwide
Website: www.vadv.org
Email: vadv@tni.net

WASHINGTON STATE **Coalition Against Domestic Violence**
101 N. Capitol Way, #302
Olympia, WA 98501
(360) 586-1022 Fax: (360) 586-1024
www.wscadv.org

WEST VIRGINA **Coalition Against Domestic Violence**
4710 Chimney Drive, #A
Charleston, WV 25302
(304) 965-3552 Fax: (304) 965-3572
Website: www.wvcadv.org

WISCONSIN **Coalition Against Domestic Violence**
307 S. Paterson Street, #1
Madison, WI 53703
(608) 255-0539 Fax: (608) 255-3560

Website: www.wcadv.org Email: wcadv@wcadv.org

WYOMING Coalition Against Domestic Violence and Sexual Assault
P.O. Box 236
409 South Fourth Street
Laramie, WY 82073
(307) 755-5481 Fax: (307) 755-5482
(800) 990-3877 Nationwide
Website: www.wyomingdvsa.org
Email: Info@mail.wyomingdvsa.org

CANADA

Toronto Rape Crisis Centre: Multicultural Women Against Rape
Tel:416-597-8808; TTY16-597-1214

VANCOUVER - Vancouver Rape Relief and Women's Shelter Crisis Line: 604- 872-8212 http://www.rapereliefshelter.bc.ca/

WILLOWDALE - Jewish Family & Child Services - 416-638-7800

WINNIPEG - Women in Second Stage Housing - St. Norbert P.O. 202,

Winnipeg, MB, R3V 1L6. Phone: 204- 275-2600 #

IRELAND

Woman's Aid National Freephone Helpline: 1800 341 900
Telephone: 01-6788858
email:info@womensaid.ie

CORK
OSS, 94 South Main Street, Cork City
Free phone: 1800 497 497

Email:advice@osscork.ie

CLARE Haven Services
Helpline : (065) 682 9777 (Refuge 24 hour service)
Tel:0656822435
Fax:0656842646
Email:manager@clarehaven.ie
Website:http://www.clarehaven.ie

DONEGAL Women's Domestic Violence Service
Helpline : 1800 262 677
Tel:074-9126267
Fax:0749127591
Email:ddvs@eircom.net
Website:http://www.donegaldomesticviolenceservice.ie

DUBLIN Aoibhneas Women's Refuge
Helpline : 01 867 0701 (24 hour service)
Tel:018670805
Fax:018670806
Email:helpline@aoibhneas.org
Website:http://www.aoibhneas.ie/

GALWAY
COPE - Waterside House Women's Refuge
Helpline : 091 565985
Tel:091565985
Fax:091564216
Email:waterside@copegalway.ie
Website:http://www.copegalway.ie

KERRY
Adapt Kerry Women's Refuge & Support Services
Helpline : 066 712 9100
Tel:0667129100
Fax:0667127836
Email:kerryrefuge@eircom.net
Website:http://www.kerryrefuge.com

LIMERICK
Adapt Services
Helpline : 1800 200 504 (includes 24 hour refuge)
Tel:061412354
Fax:061419809

Email:info@adaptservices.ie
Website:http://www.adaptservices.ie

MEATH
Meath Women's Refuge & Support Services
Helpline : 046 9022393
Tel:0469022393
Fax:0469072739
Email:mwrefuge@eircom.net
Website:http://www.womensaidmeath.ie

MONAGHAN
Tearmann Domestic Violence Services Monaghan
Helpline : 047 72311
Tel:04772749
Fax:04772455
Email:tearmanndvs@eircom.net
Website:http://www.tearmann.net

SLIGO-WEST CAVAN -LEITRIM
Domestic Violence Advocacy Service
Helpline : 071 9141515
Tel:0719141515/0719616844
Fax:0719140842
Email:infodvas@eircom.net
Website:http://www.domesticviolence.ie

WATERFORD
Oasis House Women's Refuge
Helpline : 1890 264 364
Tel:051370367
Fax:051351836
Email:oasishouse2@eircom.net

WEXFORD
Wexford Women's Refuge
Tel: 053 21876
Fax: 053 21905
Email:wexrefuge@eircom.net

WICKLOW
Bray Women's Refuge
Helpline : 01 286 6163
Tel:012866163
Fax:012863830
Email:bwr@eircom.net
Website:http://www.braywomensrefuge.com

AUSTRALIA
Domestic Violence Resource Centre Victoria (Australia)
http://www.dvrcv.org.au/
National Helpline: 1800 200 526

NEW ZEALAND
Shine(NewZealand)
http://www.2shine.org.nz/
Phone: 0508 744 633.

SOUTH AFRICA
People Opposing Women Abuse (South Africa)
http://www.stopwomenabusehelpline.org.za/
Phone: 083 7651235

ENGLAND
TheFreephone 24-hour National Domestic Violence Helpline:
08082000247.

WALES
08088010800
Llinell Gymorth Camdriniaeth yn y Cartref a Thrais Rhywiol CymruGyfan.All Wales Domestic Abuse and Sexual Violence Helpline

SCOTLAND
Scottish Domestic Abuse Helpline
0800 027 1234 - 24HR Helpline

FRANCE

Women's shelters
Phone:
+33 5 53350303
Postal Address:
Perigueux, 24000, France
Website:
www.sos-femmes-dordogne.com

SPAIN
INFORMACIÓN Y ASISTENCIA A MUJERES VÍCTIMAS DE AGRESIONES
Main Service:
Crisis support
Phone:
+34 967 240312
Postal Address:
C/ Muelle, 7-entresuelo, ALBACETE, 02001, Spain

SWITZERLAND
NOTTELEFON FÜR VERGEWALTIGTE FRAUEN
Crisis support
Rape
Sexual abuse
+41 1 2914646
P.O. Box 3344
8036
Zürich

BELGIUM
PANDORA VWZ
Helpline
Crisis support
+32 11 261060
+32 3 8994548
Katarinalaan 8 bus 33
3500
Hasselt
pandora.vwz@pandora.be

GERMANY
FRAUEN GEGEN SEXUELLE GEWALT AN FRAUEN UND MÄDCHEN E.V.
Crisis support

Helpline
+49 6221 183643 +49 6221 181622
+49 6221 378496
Alte Eppelheimer Str. 37-39
69115
Heidelberg

ITALY
ASS.NE CENTRO ANTIVIOLENZA DI PADOVA
Crisis support
+39 049 756909
Via Nazareth 25
35128
Padova

LUXEMBOURG
FONDATION PRO FAMILIA/ CENTRE FAMILIAL BETHLEHEM
+352 517272
Pro-familia@ong.lu
www.profam.org.lu

AUSTRIA
NATIONAL WOMEN'S HELPLINE
- Women's Helpline against Male Violence

0 800 222 555

POLAND
Ul. Piaskowa 9, Zielona Góra, 65-204, Poland
- National Emergency for Victims of Domestic Violence Blue Line

0 801 120 002 (hotline/Poland);
+48 22 6660559; +48 22 666 10 36
ul. Szczotkarska 48a, Warsaw, 01-382, Poland
www.niebieskalinia.pl

CROATIA
www.sosvt.hr
- SOS Telephone for Women Victims of Violence

+385 35 449726 +385 35 449180 (SOS telephone)
Augusta .enoe 4, Slavonski Brod, 35000, Croatia
www.udrugabrod.0catch.com

BOSNIA & HERZEGOVINA
SOS Hotline Sarajevo
+387 33 221886
Sarajevo, Bosnia and Herzegovina
www.smartnet.ba/sos

- Woman - SOS Hotline Mostar

+387 36 550334 +387 36 550023
Trg Ivana Krndelja 3, Mostar, 88104, Bosnia and Herzegovina

GREECE
- SOS Helpline for Victims of Domestic Violence

+30 25310 83888
Komotini, Greece

LITHUANIA
VILNIUS SHELTER FOR BATTERED WOMEN AND CHILDREN
Refuge/shelter/safe house
+370 2 333619
ndirsien@takas.lt

FINLAND
WOMEN'S LINE FINLAND
+358 943 610 08, 0800 024 00 (helpline)
+358 943 610 88
Mannerheimintie 40 A15
00100
Helsinki
www.naistenlinja.com

Sweden
- Kvinnojouren / Tjejjouren

Helpline
+46 (0)90 779700 +46 (0)90 778181 (girls helpline)
Umeå, 903 33, Sweden

NORWAY
Norwegian Leage of Women Shelters
Main Service:
Crisis support
0154 Oslo
www.norskkrisesenterforbund.no

CHAPTER 15

WHAT THE FUTURE HOLDS NOW

Well the future is a lot brighter than our past, it is as if we have been given another shot at life and in some ways we have. Throughout all the years of abuse, I never dreamed of been able to escape, I just didn't think it would happen. The only dream that I would have was that of me been the headline news after he murdered me and how my kids would suffer growing up without their mam and having to live with him and his influence for the rest of their childhood.

I am not religious but I do believe strongly in Buddhism, but that is not a religion it is a way of life. In actual fact three of us in the house all believe and try to lead our life with the simple rule, do onto others as you would like them to do onto you. It is not always possible, but I thank Buddha and my two angels every day for what I have and for keeping me alive and safe to tell my story. Jake became Buddhist after the coma and it was what saved him in life. My plan on writing the book was two- fold really, the first was to insure that I could give my kids financial security in life, not that they wouldn't have to work for what they wanted or to support themselves .But that we wouldn't be cold in the house that if they needed clothes or shoes or to go out and have fun that they could do it without feeling guilty about using the little money that we had..

I have always been a great fan of the book and teachings by Rhonda Byrne who wrote The Secret, and one night I was really struggling as to what to do, simply to get enough money to get by .I had spoken about writing a book for many years and lots of friends had joked in the past that our life should have a movie made out of it, and I could definitely see that there was nothing that hadn't been done or experienced by us .As I was reading the secret I came across the part about a man who was having difficulties, he wasn't in anyway an abuser and he decided to publish a book he had written. He was going to use what he had learned in the secret as his way of making it succeed and he did and has never looked back.

I fell asleep one night and when I woke up the next morning, not only was I certain that I had to write the book and to tell our story, I also knew the name of it and that it was going to be a huge success, I am hoping it is. When I sat down at the computer, it was like I was a machine. I didn't have to think about anything that I wanted to write, it was just going from my brain to my keypad ,it wasn't a story that I had to make up, you see it was my life so writing about it was easy.

Now my objective in life is to insure that we are all truly happy. We intend to relocate to the USA and to have Jake open up his business as he dreams of and for him to set up and operate the educational program, that he hopes will help to stop gun murders or to at least make people more aware of how dangerous these weapons are He wants to work with law enforcement agencies and eventually to have it in all states in the USA, as that is where the largest rate of gun killings is.

The basis of this program that he has come up with is unique as far as we are aware and therefor is something new for kids and teenagers in Particular, to learn from, in relation to guns and weapons in general. However he also has a dream of been a Ranger or in Law Enforcement in some form, Most of these he cannot even apply for until he is at least 20 years old .But until then he will just gain as much experience and qualifications in the relevant fields as possible. His one dream in life was to be a US Marine and I hope that he finally gets to achieve it, but if not then he will work at helping others and in protecting all, He is a protector in life and has no fear, which means that no matter what he will deal with a situation head on in order to protect the innocent.

My intention for the future is very clear to me I intend to open up a Non- Profit organization which will be based in a rural area of a Alaska, in the USA, The reason for this is that the people of Alaska gave me the strength to become a Survivor, and I want to give back to them what they gave to me, their life free from abuse. I want to eventually open a total new concept of Shelters that will cater for all victims of abuse, irrespective of their abuse and or their gender or age, as all are entitled to live a life free from pain and to be supported. Abuse is Abuse and nobody should have to live with it and keep the secret just because others are to ignorant to reach out and help them, due to stigma or taboo.

I intend to open what would be a group of totally self- contained Log Style Cabins within a central hub, which will ensure that the security of a Shelter will still prevail, but that the family or persons staying with us can do so with their own privacy. I want it to be a place where moms/dads and their children 0-18 can live in single dwelling family cabins for up to 6 months and while there learn how to safely and productively return to the real world, by obtaining counseling, job training, self-defense, and animal therapy for the children. Mandatory Personal Defense Training will be given to all, so that they never have to be a victim in life again, and can protect themselves physically. This will instill a confidence that as a victim you never had. Whether it is a man with children or a woman with children all are welcome and nobody will ever be refused our help or support and as a former Victim I know personally how hard it is for anybody to have to flee to a shelter, hence why I want to ensure that this is perhaps a new template for shelters in the future. Nolonger Victims will be the name for this as is the Facebook and Linkedin and Twitter pages as all on there are No longer Victims in life.

I intend to form a collaboration of companies airlines, train, bus, car hire etc so that the transport to this facility for those outside of the state will also be provided for free. All profits from the sale of this book will go towards the Retreat as to me it is not a shelter it is a stepping stone to your new life, a life that will be worth living and not just existing in. And in writing this book I did so to help others not to make money, so it is my way of giving back to those that gave so much to my two boys and I.

The Rural Areas of Alaska need more support and help for all victims of abuse and this is where I want to be, I don't want to work in the city but in the small communities where what I do will make a difference and I am then always available to anybody that needs me irrespective of the time whether it be day or night. Abuse doesn't have a clock in and out period, sadly it is 24/7 so I will be as I am now available when any victim needs me. Been part of a small community and supporting all victims is the best reward to me in life that I could ask for, as in doing so it is allowing me to live my dream in the one place in the world that I can call Home, as that is where I and my boys left our hearts last year, and home is where the heart is and ours is in Alaska and with her people.

I would hope that perhaps someday in the future, I might actually meet a real man and have a normal loving relationship where we grow old together and live life to the full, if I do than that is great, but if I don't then it just wasn't meant to be. One way or the other I am going to have a great time now in life, knowing that not only have I escaped after over 20 years. But that in-spite of all the abuse that we endured I have made my life a success and all without Bas.

My children are my life before any man and that will not change now or ever. Jack wants to go back to the USA he loved it there and to continue his education and eventually go to a college like Harvard he is the intelligent one in the family so that will not be a problem for him. Like most kids he changes his mind about what he wants to do but I do know that he will do something that will make a difference whether it is as he originally wanted as a Judge or in Forensics Science which he loves. But no matter what he chooses he will be a success. Personally for Jack all that I want is for him to be able to be a kid, to not live in fear of been taken, or of me been a murder victim, that he can have friends and a normal life as all kids should. This is the one thing that he can get within the USA, as we have such a support network there that we always have friends or family to be around or with.

As for Bas I don't ever want to see or hear from him. I am sure that he will be furious and disgusted that I have told all, yet it still isn't all our story, this is sadly just some of the highlights of our life of abuse for want of a better word. There is so much that I still have not written in the book, as id be writing forever, but my main point was to let him know I am free of him now and forever .I am a Survivor and will never be a Victim again.

Two of my sons are not in my life and that really kills me, however with the way Rory has turned out to be honest I don't really want him involved with me or his brothers .It is their choice as to whether or not they keep in contact with him. I will not ever stop them but I know that they are as angry and infuriated as I am with who he has become. He has lost his only real family and the man who he hated for been the abuser .is now his friend as he too has become an abuser in so many ways.

Yet he is still my son, I don't wish him harm or bad luck in life, I simply wish he would get the help he needs, before he dies a very young man. A mams love is forever, but sometimes we have to be cruel to be kind. It was too dangerous to keep Rory in our life, but perhaps one day he will return after he has received the help he so desperately needs.

Mark is doing really well and is getting to live his dream. I cannot hold that against him as he is only a child, and someday I know I will hold him in my arms again. He is a simply a victim of manipulation from Bas I should know. It would be amazing if this book was made into a film as in doing, so it would help in my eyes so many people around the world. Not everybody can get out to buy a book and when they go to a store unless it literally jumps off the shelf at them it is easy to miss. Hence them missing the information, and the story as to how they too can escape. I will never forgive Bas for stealing my son Mark, as he simply went on holidays to see him and was never returned. Why don't I fight to get him, well it is simple. As much as I love my son and it breaks my heart, he is thriving. He is the Captain of the Football Team, the Provincial Rugby team is doing really well in school and has the girlfriend that he is crazy about. I cannot take that away from him, no matter how much it hurts me. But one day he will grow up and then I hope and pray that I can hold him in my arms and tell him how much I love him and have missed him. Until then I will watch him grow up on Facebook and smile with pride at how well he is doing in life, it has to be hard for him without his brothers also.

Behind closed doors on houses, apartments, flats, basements all around the world nobody actually knows what goes on. You are allowed to see what those people want you to see ,but look into your family, your neighbors, your friends eyes, and you will see the fear, the hurt ,the suffering that as a victim they have to not only live with daily they have to hide from an entire world solely out of fear.

Take the time to look and to listen your five minutes could very well save a victims life literally. Our future is one of love, laughter and fun, no more worries, no more fear, and no more been a victim .We are the survivors and we refuse to be considered mere statistics by any government or anybody. As much as I hated our lives of abuse, I do not regret living through all the trauma and pain. It has not only made me who I am now in life, but I would not have the sons that I have if I had not of met and married my abuser.

My sole aim now in life is simple, to help as many victims of abuse to become survivors, and to wake the world up to the pandemic of Child Abuse and Domestic Violence. Nobody is excluded from this abuse, it does not matter where you live or what you have, abusers strike in all walks of life and all communities. Remember if a child says they are been abused, Listen as they do not tell lies about abuse.

Printed in Great Britain
by Amazon